COOKING
101

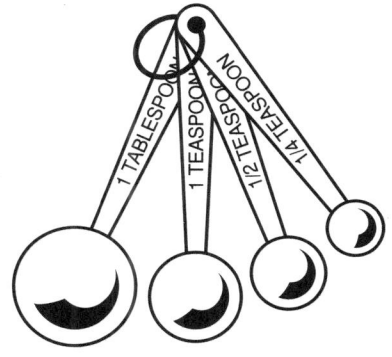

COOKING TIPS, TRICKS, FACTS & FIGURES AT YOUR FINGERTIPS.

Cooking 101

Printed in the United States of America
by Litho Printers & Bindery
Cassville, Missouri 65625

Contents

Introduction

Every cook, from the very beginner to the world's greatest chef, has something to learn. There is a wealth of information in this book for the purpose of making every cook smarter and more confident.

From how and where to store potatoes and other vegetables, to definitions of herbs and spices; this book has your answers. Many tips in this book takes into account home cooking and fresh, garden grown products and just as many more help the early learner with simple substitutions and explanations.

The purpose of this book is to give every cook, knowledge they might not have known before. The thing to remember is that all information may very due to factors such as thickness, composition, ripeness, age, quality or pan location. The more you read, the more you learn; the more one cooks, the more they enjoy experimenting and trying new recipes.

So just start cooking and enjoy yourself!

Before You Begin

EGG

1 medium egg... 2 ounces
8 to 10 medium eggs (with shells) .... 1 pound
8 to 10 egg whites .... 1 cup
10 to 14 egg yolks .... 1 cup
4 to 6 whole eggs .... 1 cup
10 average eggs without shell ....1 pound
7 to 8 large eggs without shell ....1 pound
9 to 10 medium eggs without shell ....1 pound
11 to 12 small eggs without shell ....1 pound

FLOUR

4 cups flour...1 pound
For 1 cup of sifted all-purpose flour
use any one of the following:
- 1 cup cake flour + 2 Tbsp flour
- 1/3 cup corn meal + 2/3 cup all-purpose flour
- 1/2 cup corn meal + ½ cup all purpose flour
- 3/4 cup bran + 14 cup all-purpose flour
- 1/2 cup bran + ½ cup all-purpose flour
- 1/2 cup rice flour + ½ cup all-purpose flour
- 1 cup rye flour
- 1/4 cup soybean flour + 2/3 cup all-purpose flour
- 1/3 cup soybean flour + 2/3 cup all-purpose flour
- 1/2 cup whole-wheat flour + ½ cup all-purpose flour
- ¾ cup whole-wheat flour + ¼ cup all-purpose flour

COCOA AND CHOCLOATE

For 1 ounce (square) chocolate use:

4 Tbsp. cocoa and ½ Tbsp. fat

For ¼ cup or 4 Tbsp cocoa use:

1 ounce (square) chocolate and omit ½ Tbsp fat.

4 Tbsp. cocoa ....1 ounce

4 Tbsp. cocoa .... 1 square chocolate

1 square chocolate .... 6 tablespoons

SUGAR

For 1 cup granulated sugar use:

* 1 cup brown sugar, well packed
* 3/4 cup honey and reduce liquid
* 1 ½ cups molasses and reduce liquid
* 2 cups corn syrup and reduce liquid
* 1 ½ cups maple syrup and reduce liquid

SUGAR EQUIVALENTS

2 Tbsp. sugar.. 1 ounce

2 ¼ cup granulated sugar ....1 pound

2 ¼ cup brown sugar...1 pound

GENERAL EQUIVALENTS

1 bouillon cube = 1 teaspoon beef extract

1 Tbsp cornstarch = 2/3 Tbsp. arrowroot or 1 ¾ Tbsp. wheat or rice flour

Horse-radish (1 Tbsp. fresh grated) = 2 Tbsp. bottled

1 ½ cups molasses= 1 cup sugar

1 Tbsp rennet = 1 Tbsp liquid rennet

1 ½ Tbsp quick-cooking tapioca = ¼ cup pearl tapioca (soaked at least 1 hour)

STANDARD CAN SIZES

8 oz. .... 1 cup

Picnic No. 1-East ....1 ¼ cups

12 ounces .... 1 2/3 cups

No. 300.. 1 ¾ cups

No. 1 tall... 2 cups

No. 22 .... ½ cups

No. 2 ½	3 ½ cups
No. 3	4 cups
No. 3 squat	2 ¾ cups
No. 5	7 1/3 cups
No. 10	13 cups
No. 1 square	1 pound
No. 2 ½	31 ounces

ONE POUND SHELLED NUTS EQUALS

Pounds Unshelled	*Cups, Chopped*
3 ½ pounds almonds	4 ½ cups
2 ¼ pounds filberts	3 ½ cups
1 ½ pounds peanuts	3 cups
2 ½ pounds pecans	3 cups
5 ½ pounds (black) walnuts	3 cups
2 ½ pounds (English) walnuts	4 cups

MISCELLANEOUS MEASURMENTS

4 cups flour	1 pound
2 cups rice	1 pound
2 cups chopped meat	1 pound
2 cups chopped suet	1 pound
3 cups raisins	1 pound
1 cup chopped nut	1/4 pound
2 ½ pounds unshelled pecans	1 pound shelled
1 ½ pound unshelled peanuts	1 pound shelled
2 1/3 pounds unshelled English walnuts	1 pound shelled
1 pound berry or fruit	about 2 ¼ cups
1 pound brown sugar	cups, firmly packed
1 pound cane syrup	about 1 ½ cups
1 pound confectioners' sugar	about 2 ½ cups
1 pound corn syrup	about 1 ½ cups
1 pound cube sugar	180 to 220 pieces
1 pound granulated sugar	about 2 cups
1 pound honey, strained	about 1 ½ cups
1 pound maple syrup	about 1 ½ cups
1 pound molasses	about 1 ½ cups
1 pound sorghum	about 1 ½ cups

Ingredients	*Makes About*

BEVERAGES
1 pound medium grind coffee .... 45 cups
1 pound tea .... 60 cups

CEREAL GRAINS
1 pound all-purpose flour .... 4 cups sifted
1 pound arrowroot .... 4 cups
1 pound barley flour .... 2 cups
1 pound buckwheat flour .... 4 ½ cups
1 pound cake flour .... 4 ½ cups sifted
1 pound corn flakes .... 18 cups
1 pound corn meal .... 3 cups
1 pound cornstarch .... 3 cups
1 pound cracked wheat .... 2 ¼ cups
1 pound cream of wheat .... 2 ½ cups
1 pound graham flour .... ½ cups
1 pound hominy grits .... 2 ½ cups
1 pound macaroni, broken .... 5 cups; 12 cups cooked
1 pound noodles, broken .... 5 ½ cups; 10 cups cooked
1 pound pearl barley .... 2 cups
1 pound rice .... 2 ¼ cups; 8 cups cooked
1 pound rice flour .... 4 cups
1 pound rolled oats .... 5 cups; 10 cups cooked
1 pound rye flour .... 4 ½ cups
1 pound soybean flour .... 7 ½ cups
1 pound spaghetti, broken .... 5 ½ cups; 11 cups cooked
1 pound tapioca .... 2 ½ cups

DAIRY PRODUCTS
1 pound cheese, grated .... 4 – 5 cups
1 (15-ounce) can condensed milk .... 1 1/3 cup
1 pint cream .... 2 cups
1 (14 ½ -ounce) can evaporated milk .... 1 ¾ cup
1 pint fresh milk .... 2 cups
1 pound powdered milk .... 3 cups

| | *Ingredients* | *Makes About* |

DRIED FRUITS

Ingredients	Makes About
1 pound currants	3 ½ cups
1 pound dates	2 ½ cups, pitted; 3 cups, chopped
1 pound dried apples	10 cups cooked
1 pound dried apricots	4 ½ cups cooked
1 pound dried peaches	6 cups cooked
1 pound dried prunes	4 cups cooked
1 pound figs	3 cups chopped
1 pound raisins (seeded)	2 ½ cups
(seedless)	3 cups

FRESH FRUIT

Ingredients	Makes About
1 pound apples	2 – 6 apples; 3 cups diced; 1 ½ cups sauce
1 pound apricots	8 – 14 apricots; 2 ½ cups cooked
1 medium avocado	2 cups cubed
1 pound bananas	3 bananas; 2 cups sliced
1 pint berries	2 cups
1 pound cherries	3 cups stemmed; 2 ½ cups pitted
1 pound cranberries	4 cups; 4 cups sauce
1 medium grapefruit	1 1/3 cup pulp; 1 cup juice
1 pound grapes	1 bunch; 2 cups halved
1 dozen lemons	2 ½ cups juice
1 dozen oranges	3 - 5 cups juice
1 pound peaches	4 – 6 peaches; 2 ½ cups, sliced
1 pound pears	3 – 5 pears; 2 ½ cups cooked
1 pineapple	2 ½ cups cubed
1 pound plums	12 – 20 plums; 2 cups cooked
1 pound rhubarb	4 – 8 stalks; 3 ½ cups diced; 2 cups cooked

MELONS

Ingredients	Makes About
2 pound cantaloupe	2 – 3 portions
6 – 10 pound casaba	6 – 8 portions
5 pound honeydew	5 – 6 portions
5 – 50 pound watermelon	3 – 20 portions

Ingredients	Makes About

VEGETABLE

1 pound dried beans ....2 ½ cups; 5 – 7 ½ cups cooked
1 pound split peas............................2 cups; 4 cups cooked
1 pound Jerusalem artichokes .... 3 – 4 cups cooked
1 pound asparagus.................................... 2 cups cooked,
1 pound beets .... 2 cups cooked
1 bunch broccoli................................. 1 ½ - 2 ½ pounds
1 pound Brussels sprouts .... 3 cups cooked
1 pound cabbage ....3 ½ cups shredded, 2 ½ cups cooked
1 pound carrots............................. 2 ¼ cups diced; 2 cups cooked
2 pound head cauliflower.............................. 3 cups cooked
1 ¼ pound bunch celery............... 3 cups uncooked; 2 cups cooked
4 medium ears corn...1 cup cut
1 pound eggplant ....11 (1/2 inch) slices; 4 ½ cups uncooked;
1 ¾ cups cooked
1 pound green or wax beans.......................... 3 cups cooked
1 pound kohlrabi ....4 medium kohlrabi; 2 cups cooked
1 pound fresh Lima beans .... 2/3 cup shelled
1 pound mushrooms..........................35 – 45 medium mushrooms
1 pound dry onions.......................................3 large onions
1 pound parsnips ....4 medium parsnips; 2 ½ cups cooked
1 pound peas .... 1 cup cooked
1 pound spinach or other greens .... 1 ½ - 2 cups cooked
2 pound summer squash.............................. 2 cups cooked
5 pound Hubbard squash............................. 5 cups cooked
1 ¼ pound sweet potatoes .... 2 ¾ cups cooked
1 pound tomatoes ....4 small to medium tomatoes
1 pound white turnips...............................3 – 4 medium turnips
1 pound rutabaga.................................. 2 2/3 cups cooked
1 pound white potatoes ....3 medium potatoes; 2 ½ cups cooked

MISCELLANEOUS

1 pound chocolate, grated ....3 cups
1 ounce chocolate, grated.. 3 tablespoons
1 pound cocoa ....4 cups
1 pound fat ....2 cups
1 pound coconut.........5 ½ cups shredded; 2 ½ cups fresh shredded

SUBSTITUTIONS

Substitute 1 whole egg (for thickening or baking) for 2 egg yolks. Or 2 tablespoons dried whole eggs plus 2 1/2 tablespoons water.

Substitute 1 cup butter or margarine (for shortening) for 7/8 cup lard with 1/2 teaspoon salt.

Substitute 1 square (ounce) chocolate for 3 or 4 tablespoons cocoa plus 1/2 tablespoon fat.

Substitute 1 teaspoon double-acting baking powder for 1 1/2 tea spoons phosphate baking powder. Or 2 teaspoons tartrate baking powder.

Substitute Sweet milk and baking powder (for baking) for equal amount of sour milk plus 1/2 teaspoon baking soda per cup.

Substitute 1 cup sour milk (for baking) for 1 cup sweet milk mixed with one of the following:
- 1 tablespoon vinegar.
- 1 tablespoon lemon juice.
- 1 3/4 teaspoons cream of tartar.

Substitute 1 cup whole milk for 1/2 cup evaporated milk plus 1/2 cup water. Or 4 tablespoons dry whole milk plus 1 cup water.

Substitute 1 cup skim milk for 4 tablespoons nonfat dry milk plus 1 cup water.

Substitute 1 cup cake flour, for baking for 7/8 cup all-purpose flour.

Substitute 1 cup all-purpose flour (for baking breads) for up to 1/2 cup bran, whole-wheat flour, or corn meal plus enough all-purpose flour to fill cup.

INGREDIENT SUBSTITUTION LIST

- 1 teaspoon baking powder = ¼ teaspoon baking soda plus ½ cup buttermilk or ¼ teaspoon baking soda plus 5/8 teaspoon cream of tartar

- 1 cup sifted cake flour = 7/8 cup sifted all-purpose flour or 1 cup all-purpose flour minus 1-2 table spoons

- 1 cup self-rising flour = 1 cup sifted all-purpose flour plus 1 ½ teaspoons baking   powder and ½ teaspoon salt

- 1 cup all-purpose flour = 1 cup whole wheat flour

- 1 cup honey = 1 to 1 ¼ cups sugar plus ¼ cup liquid

- 2 large eggs = 3 small eggs

- 1 medium egg = 2 egg yolks plus 1 tablespoon water (for baking)

- 1 medium egg = 2 egg yolks (in custards or cream fillings)

- 1 ounce unsweetened chocolate = 1 square or 3 tablespoons unsweetened cocoa powder plus 1 tablespoon butter or margarine

- 6 squares or 6 ounces semisweet chocolate, melted = 1 cup semi-sweet chocolate chips, melted

- 1 tablespoon cornstarch (as thickening) = 2 tablespoons flour or 2 teaspoons quick tapioca or 2 egg yolks

- 1 teaspoon lemon juice = ½ teaspoon vinegar

- 1 tablespoon fresh herbs = ½ to 1 teaspoon dried herbs

- 1 small garlic clove = 1/8 teaspoon garlic powder

- 1 pound fresh mushrooms = 3 ounces dried or 6 ounces canned

- 1 cup whipping cream, whipped = 2 cups thawed whipped topping

- 1 cup whipping cream as liquid = 1/3 cup melted butter plus 3/4 cup milk

- 1 cup light cream = 3 tablespoons melted butter plus 3/4 cup milk

- 1 cup ricotta cheese = 1 cup cottage cheese, liquid drained

- 1 cup buttermilk = 1 cup plain yogurt, stirred, or 1 tablespoon lemon juice stirred into milk to make 1 cup; let stand 5 minutes to make soured milk for baking only (never use sour milk that's been in the fridge too long; it's actually spoiled)

- 1 cup whole milk = 2 teaspoons melted butter plus 1 cup fat-free milk (or water) or equal parts evaporated milk and water or 1 cup nonfat dry milk plus 2 teaspoons melted butter

- 1 cup sour cream = 3 tablespoons melted butter stirred into 7/8 cup buttermilk, soured milk or plain yogurt

- 1 cup sour cream = 1 cup plain yogurt (but it will taste less rich from the missing fat)

- Pecans = walnuts, almonds or hazelnuts

- Chunky peanut butter = creamy peanut butter (or grind roasted peanuts in a blender with a little peanut oil)

- 1 cup bread crumbs = 3/4 cup cracker crumbs

- 1 cup butter = 1 cup margarine or 7/8 cup vegetable oil or 7/8 cup butter-flavored shortening

- 1 pound lard = 2 cups shortening

- 1 cup sugar (in baking bread) = 1 cup honey plus a pinch of baking soda

- 1 cup sugar (in baking) = 7/8 cup honey plus a pinch of baking soda

- 1 cup sugar (in main dishes) = 3/4 cup honey

- 1 cup brown sugar = 1 cup white sugar plus 2 tablespoons molasses

- 1 cup molasses (in baking) = 1 cup sugar (omit baking soda; use baking powder)

- ½ cup dry red wine or white wine = 2 tablespoons sherry or port

- 3/4 cup maple syrup = 3/4 cup maple-flavored syrup, corn syrup or 1 cup sugar and increase liquid in recipe by 3 tablespoons

- 1 teaspoon pumpkin pie spice = 1/4 teaspoon nutmeg, 1/4 teaspoon ginger, 1/2 teaspoon cinnamon

- 1 pound tomatoes = 3 medium or 3/4 cup sauce (6 ounces) or 1/4 cup paste (2 ounces)

- 8 ounces tomato sauce = 2/3 cup water plus 1/3 cup tomato paste

- 3 cups tomato juice = 2 ½ cups water plus 6 ounces tomato paste plus 3/4 teaspoon salt, dash of sugar

- 1 large marshmallow = 10 mini (dust off cornstarch from their surfaces or it might overload a recipe)

- 1 cup granulated sugar = 1 ¾ cups powdered sugar for uses other than baking

- 1/4 teaspoon powdered ginger = 1 teaspoon chopped fresh or 2 teaspoon minced crystallized

- 1 head fresh dill = 2 teaspoons dill seed

- 1 tablespoon grated fresh horseradish = 2 tablespoons bottled

- 1 teaspoon lemon juice = 1/2 teaspoon vinegar

- 1 teaspoon dry mustard = 1 tablespoon prepared mustard or 1/2 teaspoon   mustard seeds

- 1/4 cup rum = 1 teaspoon rum extract plus liquid to make 1/4 cup

- 1 teaspoon vanilla extract = 1 inch vanilla bean, split and simmered in liquid of recipe

- 1 cup wine = 13 tablespoons water, 3 tablespoons lemon juice and 1 tablespoon sugar or a little less than 1 cup apple juice plus lemon juice

- 1 cup dry bread crumbs = 3 to 4 slices bread, torn and blended

- 1 cup sweetened condensed milk = 1 cup plus 2 tablespoons dry milk powder plus ½ cup warm water plus 3/4 cup sugar and dissolve

- 1/2 teaspoon cream of tartar = 1 ½ teaspoons lemon juice or vinegar

- 1 tablespoon maple sugar = 1 tablespoon granulated sugar plus a dash of maple extract

WEIGHTS AND MEASURES

Pinch	less than 1/8 teaspoon
60 Drops	1 Teaspoon
3 Teaspoons	1 Tablespoon
2 Tablespoons	1 Fluid Ounce
4 Tablespoons	1/4 Cup
8 Tablespoons	1/2 Cup
6 Tablespoons	3/8 Cup
16 Tablespoons	1 Cup
1 Cup	1/2 Pint
2 Cup	1 Pint
2 Pints	1 Quart
4 Quarts	1 Gallon
8 Quarts	1 Peck
4 Pecks	1 Bushel
16 Ounces	1 Pound

OVEN TEMPERATURES

Very slow	250 degrees
Slow	300 degrees
Moderately slow	325 degrees
Moderate	350 degrees
Moderately hot	375 degrees
Hot	400 degrees
Very hot	450 degrees
Extremely hot	500 degrees

TO TEST OVEN TEMPERATURES WITHOUT A THERMOMETER

- Sprinkle a small amount of flour in a pan and place in heated oven.
- When flour turns into a delicate brown in 5 minutes, oven temperature is slow (250 - 325 F.)
- When flour turns golden brown in 5 minutes, oven temperature

12

is moderate (325 - 400 F.).
- When flour turns to deep brown in 5 minutes, oven temperature is hot (400 - 450 F.).
- When flour turns to deep dark brown in 3 minutes, oven temperature is very hot (450 - 500 F.).

FRIED FOODS

	TEMPERATURE OF OIL	TIME IN MINUTES
Croquettes (cooked food):	375 – 385 F.	2
Doughnuts	340 – 375 F.	2 – 3
Fritters	340 – 375 F.	2 – 5
French fried potatoes	370 – 390 F.	5 – 7
Small fish	350 – 375 F.	3 - 5

DEEP FRYING

- Fats used are olive oil, vegetable oil and lard.
- Use a deep-fat frying thermometer for testing temperature or test by browning a 1-inch cube of bread.
- Dry uncooked foods browns bread cube in 60 second.
- Wet uncooked foods browns bread cube in 20 seconds.

MISCELLANEOUS COOKING HINTS

- **To cut butter cleanly**: Cover blade of knife with waxed paper or heat in hot water.

- **To measure less than 1 cup of shortening**: Pour cold water (the amount being the Difference between the amount of shortening called for in the recipe and 1 cup) into measuring cup and add shortening until water reaches the top of cup. For example, if ¼ cup shortening is desired, pour ¾ cup cold water into cup, add shortening until water reaches top and pour off water before using shortening.

- **To clean used grease**: Add slices of potato to grease and fry until potato is brown. The potato will absorb any foreign flavors and will collect some of the sediment.

- **To decorate butter**: Dip a fork into hot water and run tines across squares of butter. Garnish with a tiny sprig of parsley.

- **To keep brown sugar from becoming hard**: Place it in a glass jar and cover tightly.

- **To moisten brown sugar which has already hardened**: Place a sliced apple or ½ an apple in with sugar or place sugar to one side in a container, arrange a slice of very moist bread on the other side; cover tightly.

- **To sprinkle sugar or sugar mixtures**: Such as sugar and spices, sugar and flour, use a salt shaker.

- **Drain deep fat fried foods:** On absorbent paper.

- **To melt chocolate:** Place on waxed paper in top of double boiler and heat until melted.

- **To shell popcorn**: Use a large grater.

- **To avoid a "boil over" while cooking macaroni or spaghetti:** Add 1 tablespoon cooking oil or shortening to the water.

- **To avoid sticking while cooking macaroni or spaghetti**: Place in a colander or sieve and place in boiling water.

- **To make rice whiter and fluffier:** Add 1 teaspoon lemon juice to each quart of water while cooking.

- **To keep corn meal from lumping**: Moisten it with cold water before adding to boiling water.

- **To make a smooth thickening of flour and water**: Place in a small jar, cover tightly and shake well.

- **To keep cooked salad dressing from curdling**: Stir the beaten eggs into the cold vinegar before cooking and cook slowly in double boiler.

- **To freshen shredded coconut:** Soak in fresh milk with a dash of sugar a few minutes before using, or place in a sieve, set over boiling water and steam until moist.

- **To keep cheese fresh**: Wrap in a cloth dampened with vinegar and store in a cool place (not in refrigerator).

- **To give doughnuts added flavor**: Place a few whole cloves or a stick of cinnamon in the grease while frying.

- **When covering jelly with paraffin**: Pour a thin layer over top of jelly, place a strong piece of string on top with end over edge of glass and pour another layer of paraffin over top. Remove paraffin with string when jelly is to be used.

- **To open fruit jars easily:** Set them upside down in hot water for a few minutes.

- **To remove odors from jars and bottles**: Pour a solution of water and dry mustard into them and let stand for several hours or use a dilute chlorine solution, then rinse in hot water.

- **Keep glass jars and covers in which salad dressing:** Is purchased. Remove pasteboard insert, wash and dry and use as containers for leftovers to be stored in refrigerator or for spices, cut onion, garlic, sugars, etc, on shelf.

- **To keep a bowl from slipping on working surface**: Place it on a folded wet towel.

- **Avoid pouring cold water into hot pans**: The sudden change of temperature will cause metals to warp.

- **To test heat of a griddle**: Place a few drops of water on griddle and if water scatters it is hot enough to brown food.

- **Use kitchen shears**: To cut parsley, diced cooked meats, dice giblets, cut crusts from bread, cut marshmallows, rhubarb, celery, etc.

- **When freezing a mousse or parfait in the refrigerator**: Line tray with waxed paper, then pour in mixture to be frozen. Allow slightly more time for freezing. Or, fill paper soufflé cups with mixture, place in freezing tray. When firmly frozen pull out at the edge, removing plaits in cup and lift out onto serving plate. Garnish before or after freezing.

REFRIGERATION

What to refrigerate and what not to

WHAT TO COOL

- Jelly: Chilled jams and jellies should be edible for 6 months.

- Mustard and ketchup: Left out, both can get moldy. Toss both after 6 months.

- Film: Chill it to stop chemicals from breaking down and dimming the colors. If you may not use it for at least 3 months, freeze it.

- Cayenne, chili powder, paprika: They lose their punch when stored at room temperature.

- Milk: Leaving milk out for just 30 minutes will cause it to spoil a day earlier than it would otherwise.

- Mixed garlic: This combo invites botulism. Always refrigerate the mixture; dispose of it after 2 days.

- Hot sauce: The spices don't act as preservatives. Dump after 1 year.

- Cream-filled baked goods: Any cream needs chilling. Eat within a week.

- Coffee beans: Chilling retains the flavor.

WHAT NOT TO COOL

- Olives and canola oil: Keep them in your pantry for 6 months. But refrigerate peanuts, macadamia and walnut oils.

- Potatoes: Chilling converts the starch to sugar, making potatoes too sweet.

- Tomatoes: Cooling destroys an enzyme that gives tomatoes their flavor. Refrigerate other vegetables, though.

- Bread: Chilling crystallizes starch, making the bread stale.

- Chocolate: A harmless white film will form.

- Garlic cloves: They'll last 2 weeks unchilled. Refrigeration weakens the flavor.

- Peanut butter: The sugar prevents bacterial growth. But chuck peanut butter after 3 months.

- Alkaline batteries: Hot or cold, they'll last 5 to 7 years.

- Fruit: Chilling stops the ripening process and dulls the flavor.

- Drugs: Chilling drugs may destroy their potency. Unless your doctor or the label says otherwise, store drugs in a cool, dry drawer or cabinet.

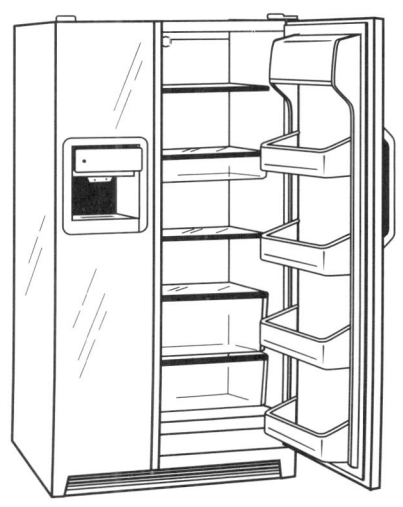

FOOD STORAGE GUIDE

Food	Storage Time	Special Handling
Baking powder or soda	18 months	Keep in airtight container after opening
Bouillon cubes, granules	1 year	
Cake mixes	1 year	
Canned foods, commercial	1 year	
Cereals	check package date	Keep in airtight container after opening.
Chocolate, baking	1 year	Keep in a cool place
Coconut	1 year	Refrigerate opened packages.
Coffee, fresh ground	2 to 3 weeks	Refrigerate or freeze opened cans or packages
Flour, all-purpose	15 months	
Flour, whole wheat	6 months	Refrigerate opened packages.
Fruit, dried	6 months	Refrigerate opened packages.
Gelatin	18 months	Keep in a dry place.
Herbs, dried	1 year	Keep in a cool, dark place. Refrigerate red spices.

Item	Time	Storage
Honey	1 year	
Jams, jellies	1 year	Refrigerate opened packages.
Macaroni, spaghetti, dried pasta	1 year	Keep in airtight container after opening.
Molasses	2 years	
Nonfat dry milk powder	6 months	Refrigerate during warm weather.
Olive oil	1 year	Keep in a tightly capped bottle away from heat & light.
Peanut butter	6 months	Refrigerate during warm weather.
Pudding mixes	1 year	
Rice, white	Indefinite	Keep in an airtight container in a cool, dry place.
Salad dressings, commercial	6 months	Refrigerate opened packages.
Shortening	8 months	Store in a cool dark place.
Sugar, brown	4 months	Keep in airtight container after opening.
Syrup (corn), maple syrup	1 year	Refrigerate maple syrup after opening.
Vegetable oil	1 year	Keep in a tightly capped bottle away from heat & light.
Yeast, active dry	check package date	Refrigerate during warm weather.

REFRIGERATOR AND FREEZER STORAGE TIMES

Food	Refrigerator	Freezer
Fresh Meat		
Chops (lamb)	3 to 5 days	4 to 6 months
Chops (pork)	3 to 5 days	4 to 6 months
Ground, stew meats	1 to 2 days	3 to 4 months
Roasts (beef)	3 to 5 days	6 to 12 months
Roasts (lamb)	3 to 5 days	4 to 6 months
Roasts (pork, veal)	3 to 5 days	4 to 6 months
Sausage (fresh pork)	1 to 2 days	1 to 2 months
Steaks	3 to 5 days	6 to 12 months
Cooked Meats		
Cooked meat, meat dishes	3 to 4 days	2 to 3 months
Processed Meats		
Bacon	1 week (open pkg.)	1 to 2 months
Hot Dogs	1 week (open pkg.)	1 to 2 months
Ham (fully cooked half)	3 to 5 days	1 to 2 months
Luncheon meats	3 to 5 days	1 to 2 months
Sausage (smoked)	1 week	1 to 2 months
Fresh Poultry		
Chicken and turkey (whole)	1 to 2 days	1 year
Chicken pieces	1 to 2 days	9 months
Duck and goose (whole)	1 to 2 days	1 year
Turkey pieces	1 to 2 days	9 months
Cooked Poultry		
Covered with broth or gravy	1 to 2 days	6 months
Pieces not in broth or gravy	3 to 4 days	4 months
Cooked casseroles	3 to 4 days	4 to 6 months
Fish	1 to 2 days	3 to 6 months
Eggs		
Whites	2 to 4 days	12 months
Whole eggs (fresh in shell)	3 weeks	Can't freeze
Yolks	2 to 4 days	12 months
Cheese		
Cottage	5 days	Can't freeze
Hard cheese	3 to 4 months	6 months
Soft cheese	2 weeks	4 months
Ice cream	Can't refrigerate	1 to 3 months
Butter, margarine	1 month	3 to 6 months

QUANTITIES TO SERVE

NUMBER OF PEOPLE	5	10	100
COFFEE	5 Tbsp.	1/2 CUP	3 pounds
SUGAR	1/2 cup	3/4 cup	3 pounds
CREAM	1 pint	1 1/2 pint	3 quarts
WHIPPING CREAM	1 cup	1 1/2 pint	4 pints
MILK	1 quart	1/2 gallon	6 gallons
FRUIT COCKTAIL	1 pound	2 pounds	2 1/2 gallons
FRUIT JUICE	1quart	2 quarts	26 pounds
TOMATO JUICE	1 quart	2 quarts	26 pounds
SOUP	1 quart	2 quarts	5 gallons
OYSTERS	1 quart	2 quarts	18 quarts
WEINERS	1 pound	2 pounds	25 pounds
MEAT LOAF	2 pounds	3 pounds	24 pounds
HAM	2 pounds	4 pounds	40 pounds
BEEF	2 pounds	4 pounds	40 pounds
ROAST PORK	2 pounds	4 pounds	40 pounds
HAMBURGER	2 pounds	4 pounds	36 pounds
POTATOES	2 pounds	4 pounds	35 pounds
SCALLOPED POTATOES	1 pound	2 pounds	5 gallons
VEGETABLES	1 pound	2 pounds	26 pounds
BAKED BEANS	1/2 pound	3/4 pound	5 gallons
BEETS	1 pound	2 pounds	30 pounds
CAULIFLOWER	1/2 pound	1 pound	18 pounds
CABBAGE FOR SLAW	1 pound	2 pounds	20 pounds
CARROTS	1 pound	2 pounds	33 pounds
BREAD	1 loaf	1 1/2 loaves	10 loaves
ROLLS	10	20	200
BUTTER	1/2 stick	1 stick	3 pounds
POTATO SALAD	1 1/2 pint	3 pints	12 quarts
FRUIT SALAD	1 quart	2 quarts	20 quarts
VEGETABLE SALAD	1 quart	2 quarts	20 quarts
LETTUCE	1/2 head	1 head	20 heads
SALAD DRESSING	1 pint	1 1/2 pint	3 quarts
PIES	1	2	18
CAKES	1	1	8
ICE CREAM	1/2 gal	1 gal	4 gallons
CHEESE	8 ounces	1 pound	3 pounds
OLIVES	6 ounces	12 ounces	1 3/4 pounds
PICKLES	1 cup	1 pint	2 quarts
NUTS	6 ounces	12 ounces	3 pounds

21

Nutrition

THE CALORIE

A calorie is a measure of the heat and energy produced by foods when used in the body. Work and play use up the energy and cold weather increases the need for heat. Calorie requirements very with types of work, age, climate and other factors.

THE NUMBER OF CALORIES
IN AVERAGE SERVINGS

FOOD	AMOUNT	CALORIES
Almonds	12 shelled	100
Almonds	5 chocolate	100
Almonds	1 cup	550
Apple	1 large	100
Apple	baked, sugared	200
Apple	brown betty 1/2 cup	250
Apple pie	1 slice	300 - 350
Applesauce	3/8 cup	100
Apple tapioca	1/2 cup	205
Apricots, cooked	3 halves with juice	100
Apricots, dried	9 halves	100
Apricots, fresh	5	100
Artichoke, French	1	158
Asparagus	10 stalks	50
Asparagus	10 stalks with butter	150
Asparagus	10 stalks with butter Hollandaise sauce	240
Asparagus soup	1/2 cup	100
Avocado	1/2 fruit	120 - 300
Bacon	4 small	100
Bacon fat	1 Tbsp.	100
Baking powder biscuits	4 small	200

Bananas	1 average	100
Beans, Lima; uncooked	1/2 cup	273
Beans, Lima; fresh	1/2 cup	100
Beans, navy; baked	1/3 cup	100
Beans, navy; dried	1/2 cup	342
Beans, soy; dried	3 1/2 Tbsp.	200
Beans, string	1/2 cup	22
Beef, corned	3 ounces	100
Beef, dried	4 thin slices	100
Beef, Hamburger steak	4 ounces	100
Beef, loaf	1 slice	100
Beef, rib	1	100
Beef, round steak	4 ounces	170 - 220
Beef steak	4 ounces	100
Beef stew	1 cup	250
Beet greens	1 cup	22
Beets	2, 2 inches in dia.	50
Blackberries, cooked with sugar	1/2 cup	200
Blackberries, fresh	25	50
Bluefish, broiled	small serving	100
Bologna	1 slice	100
Bouillon	1 cup	25
Brazil nuts	2	100
Bread, Boston brown	1 slice	52
Bread, rye	1 slice	70
Bread, white	1 slice	50
Bread, 50% whole wheat	1 slice	75
Bread crumbs, dry	1 cup	400
Bread crumbs, soft	1 cup	150
Broccoli	1 cup	45
Brussels sprouts	6	50
Butter	1 Tbsp.	100
Buttermilk	1 cup	84
Cabbage, cooked	1/2 cup	32
Cabbage, raw	1/2 cup	13
Cake, 2 egg	1 - 3/4 inch sq.	100
Cantaloupe	1/2 mellon	50
Carrots, cooked	1/2 cup	30 - 40
Cauliflower	1/2 cup	25
Celery	2/3 cup	15
Celery soup	1 cup	200
Chard, cooked	1/2 cup	36
Cheese, American	1 Tbsp.	33
Cheese	1 inch cube	70
Cheese, Cheese, cottage	5 Tbsp.	100
Cheese, full cream	1 piece	100

Cheese souffle	1/2 cup	100
Cherries	10 large	50
Chestnuts	7 average	100
Chicken, roast	4 inch slice	100
Chicken salad	1/2 cup	200
Chocolate, bitter	1 ounce	173
Chocolate, bitter	1 Tbsp. grated	29
Chocolate cake	1 small piece	200
Chocolate cream candy	average piece	80 - 100
Chocolate cream mint	1 piece	100
Chocolate drop cookie	1 piece	60
Chocolate éclair	1 piece	260 - 400
Chocolate fudge	1 inch cube	80 - 90
Chocolate malted milk	large glass	465
Chocolate, sweet, candy	1 small piece	100
Chocolate nut caramel	1 cube	100
Clams	6	50
Cocoa, powder	1 Tbsp.	40
Coconut, shredded	1 Tbsp.	34
Codfish, creamed	1/2 cup	100
Cod-liver oil	1 Tbsp.	100
Coleslaw	1/2 cup	50
Collards, cooked	1/2 cup	50
Consomme	1 cup	25
Corn bread	1 piece	120
Corn, canned	1/3 cup	100
Corn flakes	3/4 cup	100
Corn, fresh on cob	1 ear	50
Corn meal, cooked	1/3 cup	50
Corn meal, uncooked	1/2 cup	252
Corn syrup	1 Tbsp	75
Crackers, graham	2 1/2 pieces	100
Crackers, soda	2 pieces	50
Cream, heavy, 40%	1 Tbsp.	60
Cream, whipped	1 Tbsp.	35
Cream, thin, 18%	1 Tbsp.	30
Cucumber	10 inches long	50
Cup custard	1/2 cup	100
Currants, dry	1/4 cup	126
Currants, fresh	1/2 cup	34
Dates	3 - 4 pieces	100
Doughnut	1	200
Duck	4 ounces	234
Egg	1	70 - 75
Eggs, scrambled	1/4 cup	100
Eggnog	1 cup	200

Farina, cooked	3/4 cup	100
Figs, dried	1 1/2	100
Filberts	8 - 10 pieces	100
Frankfurters	1	100
French dressing	1 Tbsp.	67
Fruitcake	1 slice	100
Ginger ale	1 cup	72
Grapefruit	1/2, avg. size	100
Grapefruit, with sugar	1/2, avg. size	134
Grapefruit juice	1 cup	100
Grape juice	1/2 cup	100
Grapes	large bunch	100
Grapes, Malaga	20 - 25	100
Griddlecake	1 cake	100
Halibut, cooked	3 ounces	85 - 110
Ham	1/4 pound	270 - 400
Hard sauce	1 Tbsp.	100
Hickory nuts	1/2 cup	607
Hominy grits, cooked	1/2 cup	62
Honey	1 tsp.	25
Ice cream, vanilla	3/8 cup	100
Kale, cooked, no fat	1/2 cup	20
Kohlrabi, creamed	1/2 cup	100
Lamb chops, broiled	1 (2 inches thick)	100
Lamb, roast leg	4 ounces	225
Leeks	3 (5 inches long)	45
Lemon	1	30
Lemon juice	1 Tbsp.	5
Lemon meringue pie	1 slice, small	450
Lettuce	1/4 head	12
Lettuce with salad dressing	1/4 head	100 - 150
Liver	1/4 pound	145 - 220
Macaroni	1/2 cup	67
Macaroni with cheese	2/3 cup	200
Macaroons	each	50
Mackerel	1/4 pound	85 - 100
Maple syrup	1/2 cup	67
Marshmallows	5	100
Mayonnaise	1 Tbsp.	100
Milk, evaporated	1/2 cup	175
Milk, skim	1 cup	88
Milk, whole	1 cup	170
Mince pie	1 slice	450
Muffin	1	125 - 150
Mutton	1/4 pound	225 - 500
Napolean	average piece	453

Oats, rolled, cooked	1/2 - 3/4 cup	100
Olives	each	15
Onions, cooked	3 - 4 small	50 - 60
Orange	large	100
Orange juice	1 cup	133
Oysters,	each	6 - 16 ea.
Parsnips	1 (7 inches long)	100
Peaches, canned	1 large half with juice	50
Peaches, fresh	1 small	35
Peanuts, shelled	1/4 pound	620
Peanut butter	1 Tbsp.	100
Pears, canned	1/2 with 1 Tbsp. juice	34
Pears, fresh	1 medium	50
Peas, dried	1/4 pound	400
Peas, fresh, cooked	3/8 cup	50
Pea soup	1 cup	150
Peacans, shelled	6 nuts	100
Peppers, green	average size	20
Pineapple, canned with juice	1 slice	100
Pineapple, canned, shredded	1/4 cup	100
Pineapple, fresh	1 slice	50
Pineapple juice	1 cup	150
Plums, fresh	3 - 4 large	100
Popcorn, popped	1 1/2 cup	100
Popover	1	100
Pork	1/4 pound	300 - 620
Pork chops, broiled	1	200
Pork sausage, cooked	2 (3 inch) patties	100
Potato, white	1 average size	100
Potato chips	8 - 10 chips	100
Potato salad	1/2 cup	210
Prunes	1 average size	25
Pumpkin, cooked	1/2 cup	35
Pumpkin pie	1 slice	225
Radish	1 average size	3
Raisin pie	1 slice	450
Raisins	1/4 cup	100
Raspberries, fresh	1/2 cup	45
Rhubarb, stewed and sweetened	1/2 cup	100
Rhubarb pie	1 slice	280
Rice, steamed	1/2 cup	70
Rice pudding, plain	1/2 cup	200
Rice pudding, with egg	1/2 cup	133
Salmon, canned	1/2 cup	100
Sardines, canned	2 (3 inches long)	50
Sauerkraut	3/4 cup	25

Shrimp, without oil	each	5
Soda, chocolate	8 ounce	400
Spinach	3/4 cup	25
Spinach soup	1 cup	150
Spongecake	1 piece small	100
Squash, Hubbard, cooked	1/2 cup	50
Squash pie	1 slice	225
Strawberries, fresh	1/2 cup	50
Strawberry shortcake	average size	480
Strawberry shortcake/whipped cream	average size	530
Sugar	1 tsp.	17
Sundae, chocolate	4 ounce scoop	350
Sweet potato	1 medium	140
Tapioca cream	1/2 cup	100
Tomatoes, canned	1/2 cup	25
Tomatoes, fresh	1 large	50
Tomato juice	1 cup	50
Tomato soup	1 cup	225
Tuna, canned with oil	1/4 pound	315
Tuna, canned without oil	1/4 pound	140
Turnips	1/2 cup	25
Turnip greens	1/2 cup	35
Veal	1/4 pound	115 - 200
Waffles	1 (6 inch)	250
Walnuts, English	16 halves	100
Watercress	1/2 bunch	10
Watermelon	1 slice	100
Wheat breakfast food, dry	1 ounce	100

FOR THE SWEET TOOTH

Candy	Calories	Fat (g)
Twizzlers (1 stick)----------------------	36	0
Candy corn (10 pieces)-----------------	63	0
Smarties (15 pieces)--------------------	100	0
Tootsie Roll (1 piece)------------------	27	0.5
3 Musketeers (5.8 g.)-------------------	24	0.7
York Peppermint pattie (1)-------------	53	1
Milky Way (8.6 g.)---------------------	38	1.4
Snickers (9 g.)-------------------------	43	2.3
Twix (9.6 g.)--------------------------	50	2.3
Reese's Peanut Butter cups (7.8 g.)-----	42	2.4
Hershey's Milk Chocolate (8.4 g.)------	45	2.5
Krackel (8.4 g)------------------------	45	2.5
Nestle Crunch (10 g.)------------------	53	2.8
Mr. Goodbar (8.4 g.)------------------	45	3
Butterfinger (21 g.)--------------------	100	3.5
Almond Joy (13.6 g.)------------------	64	3.6
KitKat (15.6 g.)-----------------------	80	4
M & M's Plain (24 pieces)-------------	103	4.4
Reese's Pieces (30 pieces)-------------	113	5
M & M's Peanut (9 pieces)------------	108	5.5
Baby Ruth (28 g.)---------------------	130	6

VEGETABLE NUTRITION

VEGETABLE	calories	carb. (gm)	fiber (gm)	protein (gm)	potash (mg)	sodium (mg)	Vit.A (%DV)	Vit.C (%DV)	calcium (%DV)	iron (%DV)
Artichokes, 1 raw	60	13	7	4	470	120	4	25	6	10
Asparagus, 5 raw	25	4	2	2	230	0	10	15	2	2
Beets, 1 raw	35	8	2	1	270	65	*	6	*	4
Gr.Bell Pepper, 1 raw	30	8	2	1	210	0	15	180	*	4
Rd.Bell Pepper, 1 raw	30	8	2	1	210	0	140	380	*	4
Broccoli, 3 raw	25	5	3	3	300	25	30	140	4	4
Brussels Sprouts, 5 raw	40	9	4	3	370	25	15	130	4	8
Gn.Cabbage, raw	60	12	5	2	450	50	*	170	10	4
Rd.Cabbage, raw	50	12	4	3	410	20	*	190	10	6
Carrots, 1 raw	35	8	2	1	280	40	270	10	2	0
Cauliflower, 1/4 hd.	35	7	3	3	400	45	*	150	2	2
Celery, 1 raw	10	3	1	<1	180	50	*	8	2	*
Cilantro, raw	10	2	1	1	260	25	60	30	4	4
Collard Greens, raw	30	6	4	2	170	20	80	60	15	*
Corn, 1 ear raw	120	27	4	5	390	20	8	15	*	4
Cucumber, 1 raw	45	9	3	3	520	0	10	30	6	6
Eggplant, 1 raw	140	33	14	6	1190	15	10	15	4	8
Garlic, 2 cloves raw	10	2	<1	<1	2	0	*	4	*	*
Ginger, raw	15	4	<1	<1	105	0	*	2	*	*
Green Beans, raw	30	6	4	1	240	0	4	10	4	2
Horseradish root, 1 Tbsp.	10	2	<1	<1	85	0	*	30	*	*
Kohlrabi, raw	25	6	4	2	350	20	*	100	2	2
Leeks, 1 raw	50	13	2	1	160	20	*	20	6	10
Lettuce (Boston), 1 hd.	20	4	2	2	420	10	30	20	6	2
Lettuce (iceberg), 1/2 hd.	45	9	3	3	350	30	10	20	6	6
Lettuce, Rd. or Gr.	20	4	2	1	260	10	40	30	6	8
Lettuce (Romaine)	15	2	2	2	290	10	50	40	4	6
Mushrooms(Crimini)	10	2	0	1	220	0	*	*	*	*
Mushrooms(Enoki)	10	2	<1	<1	115	0	*	6	*	*
Mushrooms(Shiitake)	25	5	1	2	n/a	0	*	4	*	8
Mustard Greens, raw	25	5	3	3	350	25	110	120	10	8
Okra, raw	35	8	3	2	300	10	15	35	8	4
Onion(Pearl)	40	9	2	1	160	0	*	10	2	*
Onion(Red)	40	9	2	1	170	0	*	10	2	*
Onion(Yellow)	40	9	2	1	170	0	*	10	2	*
Parsley, fresh	20	4	2	2	330	35	60	130	8	20
Parsnip, raw	80	18	5	1	380	10	*	30	4	4
Potato, raw	100	26	3	4	720	0	*	45	2	6
Pumpkin, mashed	50	12	3	2	560	0	50	20	4	8
Radish, raw	5	1	n/a	<1	100	10	*	15	*	*

Rhubarb, raw	25	6	2	1	350	0	2	15	10	*
Rutabaga, raw	70	16	5	2	650	40	20	80	10	6
Scallion, raw	30	7	3	2	280	15	8	30	8	8
Snow Peas, raw	40	8	3	3	200	0	2	100	4	10
Spinach, raw	20	4	3	3	560	80	130	45	10	15
Squash(Acorn), raw	170	45	6	3	1500	15	30	80	15	15
Squash(Buttenut). Raw	60	16	5	1	490	5	220	50	6	6
Squash(Crookneck)	20	4	2	<1	210	0	6	15	2	2
Squash(Hubbard), raw	40	9	3	2	320	5	110	20	*	2
Sweet Potato, raw	130	33	4	2	350	45	440	30	2	2
Swiss Chard, raw	20	4	2	2	380	210	70	50	6	10
Taro Root	20	4	2	2	380	210	70	50	6	10
Tomato, raw	35	7	1	1	360	5	20	40	2	2
Tomato,(Cherry), raw	20	4	<1	<1	190	10	10	15	*	2
Tomato(Roma), raw	40	9	2	2	410	15	25	60	*	4
Turnip, raw	35	8	2	1	230	80	*	45	4	2
Turnip Greens, raw	25	6	3	2	300	40	150	100	20	6
Watercress, chopped	5	<1	<1	<1	110	15	30	25	4	*
Yellow Wax Beans, raw	30	7	3	2	210	5	2	25	4	6
Zucchini, raw	45	9	4	4	800	10	20	50	4	8

Yes, tomatoes are a fruit.
* Indicates less than 2% daily value
Nutritional values can vary slightly depending
on growing conditions.

VITAMINS

Vitamins are nutrients that are organic compounds which are required in tiny amounts for essential metabolic reactions. Most vi tamins can be obtained from a diet which includes a good selection of fruits and vegetables.

Vitamins have many different functions. Some function as hor mones (vitamin D), antioxidants (vitamin E), and some as mediators of cell signaling and regulators of cell and tissue growth and differ entiation (vitamin A). The largest number of vitamins (B complex) aid in metabolism.

Until the 1900's vitamins were obtained solely through food in take. Vitamins are now commercially produced and are available as inexpensive pills.

MINERALS

Minerals are chemical elements (as opposed to organic compounds, as in the case of vitamins) necessary for the health and maintenance of bodily functions. The following foods are arranged in their order of highest content for the following three minerals.

CALCIUM	IRON	PHOSPHORUS
(key for bones and teeth)	*(essential for the transfer of oxygen in the body)*	*(used in bone tissue and for energy conversion)*
Milk	Liver, beef	Liver, lean meat
cheese	heart, oysters	veal, fowl, fish
cauliflower	beef, veal	lamb, pork, beef
fresh vegetables	vegetables	glandular meats (kidney)
oysters	beans	milk, oysters, cheese
beans	lamb	beans, peas
strawberries, oranges	pork	eggs, oatmeal
almonds	fowl	fresh vegetables
eggs	eggs	brazil nuts, cashew nuts
figs, dates	molasses	almonds, peanuts
raisins, prunes	fruit, dried	filberts, bread
molasses, fish	apricots	kale, corn, raisins

FOOD LABEL MEANINGS

American Heart Association: No more than 3 grams 9g.) fat, 1 g. saturated fat 20 milligrams (mg) cholesterol, and 480 mg. sodium. Also at least 10 percent of the daily value of protein, vitamins A and C, calcium, iron or fiber.

Extra Lean: Less than 5 g. fat, 2 g. saturated fat and 9.5 mg. cholesterol per serving.

Fat-free: Less than 0.5 g. fat per serving.

Fat-free Food: Foods that are naturally fat-free, such as vegetables.

Lean: Less than 10 g. fat 4.5 g. saturated fat and 05 mg cholesterol per serving of meat or seafood.

31

Light (or "lite"):	Half the fat of the regular version, which doesn't mean it's healthy. Many light salad dressings have 6 g. of fat per tablespoon.
Low Calorie:	Fewer than 40 calories per serving.
Low Cholesterol:	No more than 20 mg. cholesterol per serving.
Lot Fat:	No more than 3 g. fat per serving.
Low Sodium:	Less than 140 mg. per serving.
May reduce the risk of heart:	Grain foods that contain at least 16 g. whole grains
Disease and certain cancers:	Contains less than 3 g. fat per serving. For cereal, the serving size is usually about 1 cup.
May reduce cholesterol:	Foods rich in soluble fiber can help lower cholesterol, so the FDA allows this claim on foods that contain 0.75 g. soluble fiber per serving.
Reduce Fat:	25 percent less fat than the regular version of the food.

ENERGY FOODS

Low Energy	Medium Energy	High Energy
All-Bran cereal	Black-bean soup	Baked potato
Apples	Cantaloupe	Carrots
Baked beans	Cheese pizza	Cornflakes
Cherries	Fresh apricots	Honey
Chocolate	Green peas	Instant mashed potatoes
Dried apricots	Ice cream	Pretzels
Flavored yogurt	Mangoes	Rice cakes
Grapefruit	Muffins	Shredded wheat
Grapes	1-minute oats	Sports drinks
Kidney beans	Orange juice	Waffles
Milk	Popcorn	Watermelons
Mixed-grain bread	Raisins	White bread
Oranges	Ripe bananas	Whole wheat bread
Pasta	Soft drinks	
Pears	Sweet potatoes	
Rice-bran cereal	Table sugar	
Sponge cake		
Tomato soup		
Unripe bananas		

Bread

TIPS ON BREAD MAKING

- Stale yeast or yeast that has been frozen causes an acetous fermentation which gives bread an unpleasant flavor.

- Never dissolve yeast in a liquid that is too warm. Soften yeast in lukewarm liquid.

- Best rising temperature for yeast dough is 85 degrees F.; above 90 degrees, growth of yeast cells will be so fast as to result in a coarse-textured bred. Below 80 degrees, yeast cells will not grow fast enough to make good bread. Even warmth throughout preparation is to be desired.

- Set oven controls and preheat oven to correct temperature before placing bread in to bake. Be sure to switch the control over to "bake". The oven should be warmer at the bottom than at the top.

- Final kneading is important. Knead to the elastic stage for fine-textured bread.

- Never open the oven door on baking bread until the dough is well set; air hitting the bread will cause an imperfect result.

- For a harder crust, let dough rise without covering. For a very tender crust, cover dough while rising.

- Always remove bread from baking pans to cool, and arrange for free air circulation so the gasses formed will quickly escape.

34

- Heavy bread is the result of kneading in too much flour or not using enough yeast.

- Yeast dough must be kneaded thoroughly to distribute the yeast cells evenly through the dough.

BREAD HINTS

- **To cut fresh bread easily**: Cut with a hot knife.

- **To make a large croustade**: For serving creamed food, cut crusts from a loaf of bread and remove center, leaving walls and bottom ¾ inch thick. Brush with butter and toast. Make small croustades from sections of loaf.

- **To butter bread for thin sandwiches**: Spread end of loaf with softened butter and cut as thin as possible. Repeat.

- **To freshen rolls**: Place in a paper bag. Twist top of bag closed and heat in hot oven (400 F.)for 15 minutes

- **To prevent toast from becoming soggy**: When used as base for poached egg, use a pierced pancake turner to remove egg from water and let drain thoroughly.

- **To prepare crumbs from dry bread**: Force through a food chopper or place dry bread in a small cloth sack and crush with a rolling pin.

- **To keep bread crumbs from scattering**: Tie a paper bag onto end of food chopper when preparing crumbs.

- **To make attractive designs on crackers**: Press cheese and smooth spreads through pastry tube or a funnel made of heavy white paper.

- **To remove pie, cake or bread pans from oven:** Use a large pancake turner, a pair of strong tongs or a pair of good potholders.

- **To prepare quick timbales:** Press thin squares of fresh bread into muffin pans and toast. The corners will turn up.

Fruits

Apples: Choose firm apples of good color and flavor. Immature apples will be poor in Color and flavor and shrivel after storage. Overripe apples are mealy and poor in flavor. Brown-tinted irregular area on surface is called scald. It is caused by gases given off by apples during storage. If slight, it affects quality very little.

Apricots: Are usually picked slightly immature. Best quality, tree-ripened cannot be shipped, so they are found only near growing areas. Select plump, firm, uniformly colored fruit. Immature fruit is greenish-yellow, hard and slightly shriveled; lacks flavor. Ripe fruit very perishable; avoid bruised fruit.

Avocados: May vary from spherical to pear-shaped, 5 ounces to 3 pounds, this smooth skin to thick rough skin, green to almost black. Shape, size and skin do not indicate quality. Select bright fresh-looking fruit just beginning to soften; avoid bruised fruit. Light brown irregular marking does not affect quality. Decay indicated by dark sunken spots.

Bananas: Have the best flavor if harvested green. Buy yellow-ripe or full-ripe fruit. Good eating quality indicated by a full yellow or red color flecked with brown. Avoid soft, mushy fruit, blackened areas or mold. Bananas that have become too cold will not ripen properly and will be of poor flavor.

Blackberries, Dewberries, Loganberries, Raspberries: Should have a bright, clean, fresh plump appearance and solid full color. Overripe berries are dull in color, soft, leaky. Leaky berries are indicated by staining the inside of the container.

Blueberries, Dewberries, Loganberries, Raspberries: Select plump, fresh looking, clean and dry berries that are free from trash. Deep full color indicates good quality; mold indicates decay. Moisture indicates breakdown of fruit. Overripe fruit is dull and lifeless. Berries held long after picking are dull and shriveled.

Cherries: Select sweet cherries for eating and tart cherries for cooking. Bright fresh appearance, plumpness and good color indicate good quality. Unripe fruit is small, hard, poor in color, usually acid. Overripe fruit is soft, dull in color, shriveled and leaky. Avoid bruised fruit and fruit with small brown, circular spots.

Cranberries: Should have fresh, plump appearance, firmness and luster to indicate good quality. Avoid shriveled, dull, soft or moist berries.

Fresh Figs: Choose fully ripe and soft figs. Color and size depend upon; variety. Ripe figs sour and ferment quickly. Odor indicates souring. Avoid bruised fruit.

Grapefruit: Russet on fruit does not affect flavor. The fruit should be firm and springy, not soft or flabby and should be heavy for their size. Decay is indicated by soft discolored area at button end.

Grapes: Grapes to be served on the stem should be firm, highly-colored and should adhere to the stem. For juice, ripeness is essential but compactness or shattering from stem are not important. Frozen grapes have poor flavor; indicated by dullness, stickiness, shattering from stem. Decay indicated by mold, wet berries and stained containers.

Lemons: Select heavy ones with smooth-textured skins. Avoid decay at stem end or soft, spongy fruit.

Limes: Select green, heavy fruit. Surface blemishes do not indicate poor fruit. Yellow fruit is not acid enough.

Oranges: Select firm, heavy fruit. Surface blemishes do not affect fruit. Avoid light, puffy fruit with badly creased skins.

Peaches: Should be free from blemishes, firm, fresh-appearing with whitish or yellowish ground color. Green ground color indicates fruit was picked too soon to allow ripening. Select overripe fruit only for immediate consumption. Worminess is shown by small holes from which gum exudes. Decay (brown circular spots) spreads rapidly.

Pears: Firm, not hard, free from blemish, clean, not misshapen, wilted or shriveled. Soft at base of stem, for immediate consumption. Wilted or shriveled fruits have been picked too early and will never ripen or have good flavor. Avoid fruit with water-soaked appearance.

Pineapples: Are picked in slightly immature state. Ripe pineapple has a dark orange- yellow color and a fragrant odor and the eyes are flat. Select fruit relatively heavy for its size. If picked when too immature fruit will not ripen, will be dull and lifeless, often yellow, eyes poorly developed, pointed. Avoid bruised fruit. Fruit losses moisture if held a long time, shrinks in size, color darkens. Decays rapidly; look for dark areas at base or around eyes, sour odor, mold, moisture. Light-colored area on side indicates sunburn; fruit will be hard, dry and pithy.

Plums and prunes: Ripe fruit is plump and yields too slight pressure. Immature fruit is hard, shriveled, and poor in color and flavor. Over-mature fruit is soft, leaky and insipid. Brownish color on side indicates sunburn and the flavor is likely to be poor.

Quinces: Good fruit is hard, free from blemish and is greenish-yellow. Immature fruit is green and lacks flavor.

Rhubarb: Choose fresh, firm, crisp, tender, thick stalks (red or pink).

Strawberries: Choose bright, clean berries of solid red color and with caps attached. Small, misshapen berries have poor flavor and often have small hard green areas.

MELONS:

Cantaloupes: Scar at stem end should be slightly sunken and calloused. Do not depend on softening at stem end; repeated pressure will produce this on immature fruit. Pronounced yellowing indicates over-ripeness. Netting should be coarse, corky and grayish. Avoid bruised or flabby fruit. Decay shows as soft sunken spots, mold or moisture at stem end.

Casaba: Select melon of yellow-colored rind, softening at blossom end. Immaturity is shown by firmness and greenish-white color; decay by dark sunken areas.

Honey Ball or Honeydew: Choose a melon with rind of light yellow which yields slightly to pressure. Dark sunken spots show decay. Flavor will be good if spots have not penetrated rind. Greenish-white color and hardness show immaturity.

Watermelons: Should be firm, symmetrical, fresh, good color, a bloom on surface, lower side yellowish. Immature melons are hard, unripe in appearance, underside is white or pale green. Over-mature melons are dull, lifeless and feel springy to touch. Misshapen melons are usually of poor quality. Worm injury is shown as healed punctures or burrows. Decay occurs at stem and spreads rapidly. Decay at blossom end is shown by a flat, dry, leathery spot. Dark, sunken, watery spots on body of melon do not affect quality if flesh is not penetrated.

- **To make orange or grapefruit segments**: Pare with a sharp knife, slide knife blade along each segment wall to center and turn out segment with a slight twist of the knife.

- **To peel grapefruit and oranges easily**: Let them stand in boiling water about 8 minutes before peeling.

- **To keep lemons fresh**: Place in glass jar, fill with water and cover tightly.

- **To obtain most juice from lemons**: heat before squeezing.

- **To extract juice from lemon when a small amount is needed:** Puncture the skin with a fork and gently squeeze out the amount required.

- **To keep limes fresh:** Place them in a jar, cover and store in refrigerator.

- **To avoid wrinkled skins on baked apples**: Slit in a few places before baking.

- **To keep cut fruits from discoloring**: Sprinkle lemon or pineapple juice over them.

- **To prevent dried fruits from clogging the food chopper:** Add a few droops of lemon juice before grinding.

- **To keep juice in fruit which has been cut:** Cover exposed part with waxed paper and place fruit cut-side down on a dish, or fit with a transparent bowl cover and leave cut side up.

- **Wash berries:** Before hulling to retain juice.

CARE OF FRESH FRUITS

- Highly perishable fruits such as berries, cherries and plums should be placed in the refrigerator without washing and as soon as received from the market.
- Place fruit in a colander and wash with a spray.
- Firm fruit (such as peaches, apples, pears, etc.) may be washed by lightly rubbing in water.

VARIETY OF APPLES

VARIETY	SEASON	EATING	COOKING	SAUCE	PIE	JUICE
Gala	August, September	x	x	Best	x	x
PaulaRed	September	x	x	x	x	
McIntosh	September	x		Good		x
Honeycrisp	September	x	x	Good	x	Best
Jonathan	September	x	x	V.Good	x	x
Golden Delicious	September	x	x	V.Good	x	x
Ultra Gold	September	x	x	x	x	x
Cortland	September	x		x	x	x
Jonaclicious	September	x	x	V.Good	x	x
Red Delicious	September	x		Good		
Jonagold	September	x		Good		x
Jubilee	September,October	x	x	x	x	
Keepsake	September,October	x	x		x	
Shizuka	September,October	x	x	x	x	x
Rome	October		x		x	
Sundance	October	x	x			x
Blushing Gold	October	x	x		x	x
Enterprise	October	x	x			
Melrose	October	x	x	V.Good	x	x
Stayman Winesap	October	x	x	Good		x
Granny Smith	October	x	x			x
Pink Lady	October	x	x	Good	x	x
Suncrisp	October	x	x		x	x
Fuji	October	x	x	Best	x	
Arkansas Black	October		Baking	too hard		

TYPES OF CITRUS FRUIT

Most Common

Clementine	Mandarin	Lemon	Lime
Leech	Tangerine	Orange	Satsuma
Lime	Kumquat	Ugli	
Sweety	Minneola	Rough Lemon	
Grapefruit	Tangelo	Pummelo	

Citrus is a flowering plant originating in tropical and subtropical Southeast Asia. Presently grown in South America, Mexico and the southern portion of the Unite States, the fruit is commercially important to be eaten fresh or for its juice.

Citrus fruits are notable for their fragrance, flavor and juice which contain a high quantity of citric acid.

It also has many medical uses; lemon juice is used to relieve the pain of bee stings. The orange is also used in vitamin C pills, which prevents scurvy.

Vegetables

Globe Artichokes: Select compact, heavy, plump globe; large, clinging, fleshy leaf scales; good green color. Age or injury produces brown color. Over-mature artichokes are open, centers may be fuzzy or purple, tips of scales hard and woody. Flavor will be strong, scales woody. Look for worm injury at base of bud.

Asparagus: Select fresh, tender and firm with close compact tips. Wilted stalks with spreading tip indicate long time has elapsed since cutting. Angular stalks are likely to be woody.

Lima Beans: Pods should be well-filled, bright and dark green. Shelled beans should be plump, tender-skinned and greenish-white. Avoid dried, shriveled, spotted, yellow or flabby pods. Test shelled beans for tenderness.

Beets: Should be smooth and free from blemish. Avoid shriveled beets. Beets which have been left too long in the field will have short necks covered with leaf scars.

Broccoli: Should be fresh, clean and not over-mature. Select stalks that are tender and firm and heads compact with no evidence of flowering. Yellowing leaves may indicate woodiness. An occasional opened blossom does not indicate over- maturity.

Brussels Sprouts: Select sprouts that are firm and compact and have a fresh green color. Puffy sprouts are of poor quality. Worm injury may cause considerable waste. Smudgy dirty appearance may indicate the presence of plant lice.

Cabbage; Select reasonably solid heads with all but 3 or 4 wrapper leaves removed and stem cut close to the head. Early cabbage will not be as firm as winter cabbage. Avoid worm injury, decay, yellowing of leaves, bursting heads. Cabbage only slightly affected can be trimmed and used to advantage. If base of some of outer leaves have separated from stem, cabbage may be strong flavored and coarse.

Carrots: Select firm, fresh, smooth and well-shaped carrots with good color. Avoid wilted, shriveled, cracked, excessively forked carrots. Excessive masses of leaf stems indicate large cores.

Cauliflower: Choose white, clean, firm, compact heads. Avoid spreading flower clusters, spotted or bruised curd.

Celery: Should be brittle enough to snap easily. Avoid pithy, stringy stalks detected by pressure Open head to detect rot, insect injury and seed stem formation.

Chard: Leaves should be crisp, tender and free from insect injury.

Chayote: Varies greatly in size and shape. Select firm fruit.

Chicory, Endive, Escarole: Should be crisp, fresh and tender. Tough coarse-leaved plants may be bitter.

Collards: Are similar to kale. Leaves should be large and curled at edges.

Corn: Field corn may be as tender as sweet corn but not as sweet. Sweet corn is usually smaller, husks are darker green, ribbon-like ends hang free. Dry, straw-colored husks are an indication of age or damage. Immature corn lacks flavor. Worm injury confined to tips can be cut out with little waste.

Cucumbers: Should be firm, fresh, well-shaped and a deep green color. Shriveled, withered cucumbers are rubbery and bitter. Over-maturity is shown by puffiness, yellowing; flesh rubbery and seeds hard. These are not suitable for slicing but excellent for some kinds of pickles.

Dandelions: Select large, tender, fresh green plants before the plant begins to flower.

Dasheens: Tubers are small; scars are natural, not blemishes.

Eggplant: Should be heavy, firm, free from blemish and a uniform dark color. Wilted, shriveled, soft or flabby eggplants are often bitter.

Fennel: Select crisp bulbs and stalks.

Garlic: Should be dry and not soft or spongy, outer covering unbroken. Avoid dirty bulbs.

Kale: Should be dark or bluish-green color, clean and fresh. Avoid wilted or yellow leaves.

Kohlrabi: Select small bulbs without woody tops.

Lettuce: Head lettuce should be fresh, crisp, tender, firm, and free from decay and should not have excess covering leaves. Seed stem (knob-like swelling beyond normal contours) indicates bitter flavor. Dead or discolored areas may indicate decay. Wilted outer leaves do not affect interior. Leaf lettuce should be crisp.

Mushrooms: Select firm mushrooms with no mold or softness.

Mustard Greens: Should be fresh, tender, crisp and a full green color. Wilted, dirty, spotted leaves show age. Do not select those with seed stems.

Okra; Choose fresh, tender pods that will snap easily. Dull dry appearance shows hard, woody, fibrous texture with hard seeds. If shriveled or discolored, okra will lack flavor.

Dry Onions: Should be bright, clean, hard and well-shaped with dry skins. Avoid developed seed stem or sprouts. Moisture at neck indicates decay.

Green Onions: Should have green fresh tops, well blanched 2 to 3 inches from root. They should be young, crisp and tender. Wilting and yellowing of top may indicate age or too long a period since pulling.

Parsley: Select bright, green, fresh parsley free from yellowed leaves. Slightly wilted stock may be revived in ice water or in a covered container or the refrigerator.

Parsnips: Select smooth, firm parsnips of medium size. Soft, flabby roots are pithy and fibrous. Large roots will have woody cores. Softness may mean decay.

Peas: Should be young, fresh, tender and sweet. Pod should be bright green, slightly velvety, fresh-picked. Flat, dark, green pods indicate immature peas. Swollen pods of poor color flecked with grey specks indicate an advanced stage of maturity. Peas will be tough, flavor poor. Avoid wet and mildewed pods.

Peppers: Select firm, thick-fleshed, well-shaped peppers of fresh appearance. Immature peppers are soft, pliable, thin-fleshed, pale. Avoid shriveled, limp or pliable peppers or those with surface blemishes.

Potatoes: Should be sound, smooth, shallow-eyed and reasonably clean. Select size according to use intended. Avoid leathery, wilted, discolored potatoes. Green color is sunburn and gives bitter taste. Hallow heart or blackheart can be found only by cutting. It is more likely to be found in very large potatoes. Frozen potatoes may be wet, have dark rings below surface and turn black on cooking. If a quantity is bought sort into similar sizes to insure uniform cooking.

Rutabagas: Often coated with wax to preserve freshness. If not coated, select rutabagas that are firm and unwrinkled.

Radishes: Select smooth, tender, crisp radishes, mild in flavor. Leaves are not indication of quality. Avoid pithy, spongy radishes.

Salsify (Oyster Plant): Choose smooth firm roots of medium size. Soft, flabby roots will be pithy and fibrous. Woody cores will be found in large roots.

Spinach: Should be well-developed stocky plants with fresh, crisp and clean leaves. Small, straggly or overgrown stocky plants are often tough. Watch for seed stems and soft slimy rot.

Squash: Summer squash should be fresh, heavy for size, free from blemish, rind easily punctured. Winter squash should be heavy, free from blemish with the rind hard.

Sweet Potatoes: Should be smooth, well-shaped and unblemished. Misshapen, cracked potatoes are undesirable only because of waste. Decay may be a soft wet or a dry shriveled sunken dis colored area. Small dark clay-colored spots uniting to form large dark blotches are only skin deep. Damp potatoes may have been badly frozen.

Tomatoes: Should be mature, firm, plump, smooth, good color and free from blemishes. Cracked tomatoes must be used at once.

Turnip Tops: Be sure they are fresh, clean, crisp and tender. Examine for plant lice.

Turnips: Select smooth, firm turnips with only a few leaf scars around crown. Tops should be fresh, green and young.

Zucchini: Select small crisp zucchini. Wilted zucchini will have poor flavor.

VEGETABLE HINTS

- **To score cucumbers**: Mark lengthwise with tines of fork and cut slices crosswise. Flute peeled bananas in the same way.

- **Grease potato skins before baking**: To keep them soft and ten der.

- **To keep sweet potatoes and apples from turning black**: Place them in salted water at once after paring.

- **Peel onions**: Under water to keep them from affecting eyes.

- **To prevent odor of cooking onions and cabbage**: Add 1 table spoon lemon juice or wedge of lemon with skin on.

- **To extract juice from onion**: Cut a slice from root end and scrape juice from center with edge of a teaspoon.

- **To mince onion and other vegetables**: Peel, cut off a slice, cut exposed surface of onion Into 1/8 inch squares and as deep as needed. Slice thinly.

- **To keep fresh parsley, mint and watercress**: Wash thoroughly, shake off excess water, place in a glass jar, cover and place in refrigerator.

- **To remove vegetable stains from hands**: Rub them with a slice of lemon.

- **To make celery curls**: Cut stalks lengthwise into thin strips to within 1 inch of the end and place in ice water. Longer stalks may be curled at both ends.

- **For delicious and crisp celery**: Let stand in cold water to which 1 teaspoon sugar per quart has been added.

- **To separate lettuce leaves easily**: Cut out core and place lettuce head under running water so that it runs into cavity. Drain and dry leaves before using.

- **To garnish lettuce leaves**: Place paprika on waxed paper and dip edges of leaves into it.

- **To freshen asparagus:** Set stems in cold water.

- **To freshen withered parsnips, carrots, potatoes, cabbage, lettuce, etc**: Let stand in very cold salted water.

- **To remove the skins from carrots easily**: Drop into boiling water and let stand for a few minutes.

- **To keep cauliflower white while cooking**: Use ½ milk and ½ water and cook without covering, until just tender.

- **To restore sweetness in old vegetables**: Add a little sugar to water while cooking.

- **To skin a tomato easily**: Place a fork through the stem end, plunge into boiling water and then into cold water. Or hold over direct heat. Break skin at bottom end and peel skin back.

- **To keep leftover canned pimientos from spoiling**: Place in a small dish and cover with cooking oil.

PREPARING VEGETABLES

- Wash and scrub vegetables and remove waste (leaves, roots, etc.).

- Shake as much of the water as possible from the vegetables and place them in the refrigerator vegetable drawer, covered con tainers, glass jars or in food storage bags.

- Even lettuce that is quite wilted will freshen in 10 -12 hours.

- Root vegetables may be freshened in salted ice water.

- When harvested, root vegetables may be stored in a cool dark place for many months, either in a stone far or covered with sand or earth. Sprinkle the earth with water once each month.

CARE OF FRESH VEGETABLES

Cooking vegetables causes them to lose vitamins, minerals, col or and flavor if not cooked correctly. Here is a list of healthy way to cook vegetables.

Steaming: Is fast, preserves nutrients, and works best for fresh and frozen vegetables.

Roasting: Cooking with Olive Oil is quick, simple, and is an excellent way to cook vegetables to preserve the vitamins, flavors and minerals.

Stir-Frying: Frying sliced vegetables in any liquid, such as chicken broth or seasonedliquid, until they are crisp and glossy.

VEGETABLE PLANTING AND STORAGE GUIDE

Vegetable	Approximate planting date	Number of plants per family (of 4)	Distance between rows	Storage temperature	Storage time (in weeks)	How to preserve
Attichoke	April-June	3 to 4 plants	48" - 60"	32 F.	1 to 2	Freeze, can or dry
Asparagus	Feb.-March	30 to 40 plants	60"	32 F.	3 to 4	can, dry or freeze
Beans, bush	April-May	15 to 25 ft. row	30"	40 F.	1 to 3	can, dry or freeze
Beans, pole	May	15 to 25 ft. row	30"	40 F.	1 to 3	can, dry or freeze
Beets	April	10 t015 ft. row	18"	32 F.	3 to 10	can, dry or freeze
Broccolli	April-May	15 to 20 ft. row	36"	32 F.	1 to 2	dry or freeze
Brussels sprouts	May-July	15 to 20 ft. row	36"	32 F.	3 to 4	dry or freeze
Cabbage	April	10 to 15 ft. row	36"	32 F.	12 to 16	dry or freeze
Cantaloupes (mellons)	May	5 to 10 hills	72"	40 - 50 F.	2 to 4	dry or freeze
Carrots	March-July	20 to 30 ft. row	24"	32 F.	16 - 20	freeze
Cauliflower	April-July	10 to 15 plants	36"	32 F.	2 to 3	can, dry or freeze
Celery	March	20 to 30 ft row	24"	32 F.	8 to 16	pickle, dry or freeze
Chard	April-July	3 to 4 plants	30"	32 F.	1 to2	freeze
Chives	March-May	1 clump	0	0	0	can, dry or freeze
Corn, sweet	May	20 - 30 feet	36"	32 F.	1/2 to 1	can, dry or freeze
Cucumbers	May-June	6 plants	48"	45 - 55 F.	2-Jan	freeze, pickle or puree
Eggplant	May	4 to 6 plants	36"	50 - 60 F.	1 to 2	dry or freeze
Endive	April-August	10 to 15 ft. row	24"	32 F.	2 to 3	use fresh
Garlic	Sept.-Feb.	10 to 20 ft. row	18"	65 - 70 F.	24 - 32	use fresh
Kohlrabi	April-August	10 to 15 ft. row	24"	32 F.	2 to 4	use fresh
Leeks	March-May	10 ft. row	24"	32 F.	4 to 12	use fresh
Lettuce	April	10 to 15 ft. row	24"	32 F.	2 to 3	use fresh

Vegetable	Approximate planting date	Number of plants per family (of 4)	Distance between rows	Storage temperature	Storage time (in weeks)	How to preserve
Mustard	April	10 ft. row	24"	32 F.	1 to 2	use fresh
Okra	May	10 to 20 ft. row	36"	32 F.	50 to 60	use fresh
Onions	"sets" in April	30 to 40 ft.row	18"	32 - 36 F.	12 to 32	can, dry or freeze
Onions, green	April-May	0	0	85 - 90 F.	0	use fresh
Parsley	March-June	1 to 2 plants	24"	32 F.	1 to 2	dry or freeze
Parsnips	April-May	10 to 15 ft row	24"	32 F.	8 to 16	freeze
Peas	Feb.-May	30 to 40 ft.row	36 bush	32 F.	1 to 2	can, dry or freeze
Peppers	May-June	5 to 10 plants	36"	45 - 55 F.	4 to 6	can, dry or freeze
Potatoes, sweet	May	50 to 100 ft. row	36"	55 - 60 F.	8 to 24	can, dry or freeze
Potatoes, white	April-May	50 to 100 ft. row	30"	40 - 45 F.	12 to 20	can, dry or freeze
Pumpkins	May	1 to 3 plants	72"	55 F.	8 to 24	can, dry or freeze
Radish	April	4 ft. row	6"	32 F.	0	use fresh
Rhubarb	March-April	2 to 3 plants	48"	32 F.	2 to 3	can or freeze
Rutabaga	June-July	10 to 15 ft. row	6"	32 F.	8 to 16	freeze
Spinach	April	10 to 20 ft. row	18"	32 F.	1 to 2	dry or freeze
Squash, summer	May-JUne	2 to 4 plants	48"	50 - 55 F.	2 to 3	can, dry or freeze
Squash, winter	May	2 to 4 plants	72"	55 F.	8 to 24	can, dry or freeze
Tomatoes	May	10 to 20 plants	36" to 60"	55 to 65 F.	1 to 2	can, dry or freeze
Turnips	April	10 to 15 ft. row	18"	32 F.	8 to 12	can
Watermelons	May	6 plants	72"	40 F.	2 to 3	freeze

Eggs

The color of an egg's shell is determined by the breed of the bird and has nothing to do with the quality of the egg.

The color of the yolk is determined by the diet of the hens, and there is no relationship between the color of the yolk and the color of the shell.

EGG HINTS

- **To hard-cook egg yolks:** Drop into simmering water and keep below boiling until firm.

- **To divide an egg**: Beat slightly and measure with tablespoon.

- **To hold eggs together while poaching:** Add a few drops of vinegar to lemon juice to the cooking water.

- **To cut hard-cook eggs without breaking the yolk**: Dip the knife into water.

- **To prevent meringue on pies from shrinking**: Spread meringue on filling so that it touches the sides of pastry all around the edge. Bake 15 to 20 minutes in a slow oven (325 F.).

- **To glaze the top of rolls, pastry, etc**: Brush before baking with slightly beaten egg white and 1 tablespoon milk or water; use whole egg for yellow glaze.

- **To separate an egg**: Break the egg shell; hold the shell upright and catch the yolk in the bottom half of the shell and allow the egg white to run into a small bowl.

CARE OF EGGS

- Place eggs in a wire basket or other appropriate container in the refrigerator. If they are to be kept for a number of weeks place eggs on their large end for storing.

- To keep whites after eggs have been broken and separated place them in a glass jar, cover and store in the refrigerator.

- To keep yolks after eggs have been broken and separated place them in a narrow or tall glass container, cover with water or milk, then cover jar and place in the refrigerator.

- Remove eggs from the refrigerator long enough before using so they will become warmed to room temperature.

- Eggs are most easily separated as soon as they are removed from the refrigerator.

COOKING EGGS

Since eggs are toughened by high heat they should be cooked at low temperatures. Place custards, soufflés and similar egg dishes in a pan of water when baking to prevent overheating of the egg mixture. Cook egg sauces over hot water.

COOKING EGGS IN THE SHELL:

Eggs in the shell should NOT be cooked in boiling water. When eggs are hard-cooked in boiling water they are likely to be tough and leathery, while soft-cooked eggs are unevenly cooked.

Method 1: Place eggs in saucepan, cover with cold water and heat slowly to boiling.
- For soft-cooked eggs: Remove when water starts to boil.
- For hard-cooked eggs: Reduce heat and simmer 5 to 8 minutes.

Method 2: Heat to boiling, enough water to cover eggs 1 inch deep. Lower eggs into water and remove pan from heat.
- For soft-cooked eggs: Allow to remain in water 6 minutes
- For hard-cooked eggs: Allow to remain in water 25 minutes.

Method 3: Pour hot water into both parts of a double boiler. When water in the lower part boils, place eggs in top. When cooked by this method the temperature cannot reach the boiling point and eggs will cook evenly.

- For soft cooked eggs: cook 12 to 15 minutes.
- For hard-cooked eggs: cook 25 to 30 minutes.

Meat, Poultry & Fish

CUTS OF MEAT: A BASIC UNDERSTANDING

BEEF CUTS: Meat from a steer or heifer is referred to a beef.

1. Round: Slow-cooking steaks, roasts
2. Loin: Sirloin, porterhouse and club steaks
3. Ribs: Standing and rolled rib roasts
4. Flank: Steaks or stew meat
5. Chuck or shoulder: Pot roast and slow-cooking steaks
6. Plate: Corned beef, stew meat, short ribs
7. Shank: Soups and stews

PORK CUTS: Although pork is almost always tender, all pork must be cooked to the well-done stage.

1. Ham
2. Fat back: Salt pork, lard
3. Pork loins: Chops and roasts
4. Bacon
5. Spareribs
6. Shoulder butt
7. Picnic shoulder
8. Pork hock
9. Jowl butt
10. Front foot

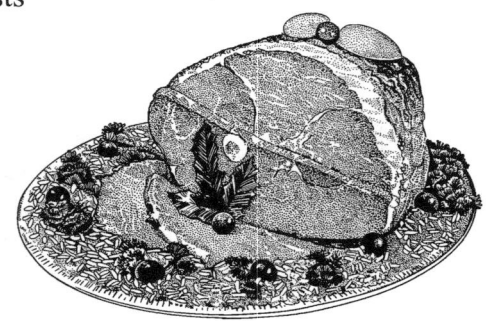

VEAL CUTS: There are 4 types: Bob Veal (up to 150 pounds), Formula-Fed or "Milk Fed" Veal (fed only a milk formula up to 450 – 500 pounds), Non- Formula or "grain-fed" Veal (calves fed solid foods in addition to milk up to 650 – 700 pounds), Rose Veal is from calves reared on farms in association with the UK RSPCA's stringent Freedom Foods program.

1. Leg: Roasts, steaks
2. Loin: Chops, steaks
3. Rib: Roasts, chops
4. Breast and Shank: Roasts, stew
5. Shoulder: Roasts, chops

LAMB CUTS: Lamb is the young of the sheep, usually brought to the market up to a year old and weighing between 30 and 50 pounds.

1. Leg: Roasts, steaks
2. Loin: Roasts, chops
3. Rib: Roasts, chops
4. Breast: Roasts
5. Neck: Braising, broth, stew
6. Shoulder: Roasts, steaks
7. Shank: Broth, stew

POULTRY: Is a term used to describe domesticated birds used for meat, eggs, or feathers. It includes chickens, turkeys, ducks, geese, pigeons, doves and game birds such as quail and pheasant.

Cuts are usually divided into two categories: white and dark meat.

1. Breast
2. Thigh
3. Drumstick
4. Wing

CARE OF MEAT

FRESH UNCOOKED MEAT
- Remove from wrapping paper.
- Wipe with a damp cloth.
- Store in the meat compartment of the refrigerator or on a platter and seal in a refrigerator storage bag.

COOKED MEAT
- Remove from wrapping paper.
- Store in the refrigerator in the meat compartment or in refrigerator storage bag

CARE OF POULTRY

WHOLE CHICKEN *Information provided covers both market birds and birds grown at home.*
- Remove from wrapping paper. Wipe inside of bird with damp cloth, making sure that it has been properly cleaned.
- If wing tip feathers have been left on, dip them into boiling water for a few minutes and pull feathers out with pliers.
- Remove all pinfeathers with tweezers. Singe over direct heat to remove fine hairs.
- Remove oil sack from tail. Wash outside thoroughly, using a soft brush and salt, corn meal, soda or soap. Rinse thoroughly and dry. Stuff and truss if to be roasted.
- Store in refrigerator, breast side down in storage bag or in a covered meat compartment.

CUT-UP CHICKEN
- Remove from paper and wash quickly but thoroughly under running water.
- Drain well, dry and store in the refrigerator in the meat compartment or in a refrigerator storage bag.
- Care for ducks, turkeys, geese and game birds are the same as for chicken.

MEAT HINTS

- **Meat or chicken may be floured easily**: By placing in a paper bag with flour and shaking well.

- **To keep bacon from curling**: Snip edges with shears before cooking or broil between racks.

- **To keep bones on crown roasts from burning**: Place in pan with bones down or spear ends of bones with fat meat.

- **When preparing small bits of meat**: Place them on skewers.

MEAT THERMOMETER READINGS

For Low-Temperature Roasting

Beef - rare .... 140 degrees F.

       medium .... 160 degrees F.

       well done .... 170 degrees F.

Pork - fresh (always well done) .... 185 degrees F.

       cured .... 160 degrees F.

       tender .... 145 to 150 degrees F.

Lamb .... 180 degrees F.

Veal .... 170 degrees F.

TEMPERATURES FOR ROASTING MEATS

Roasting meat at a constant low temperature of 325° F. (or 360° F. for pork) gives better results than by searing at a high temperature and then finishing the roasting at a low temperature. The searing does not retain the juices as was once thought and causes excessive shrinkage. Use any shallow pan large enough to hold the meat and place a wire rack in the bottom to hold the meat up out of the juices and to allow the heat to penetrate evenly from all sides.

SUGGESTED MEAT GARNISHES

Meal	Garnish
Fillets, steak, kidneys and game	Triangles of toast, fried in garlic butter
Veal, liver, kidneys and game	Lemon wedges dusted with paprika or dipped in minced parsley
Pork, ham and veal	Unpeeled, corned apple rings dusted with flour and fried in butter or bacon
Ham, meat loaf and luncheon loaf	Pineapple rings brushed with butter and broiled
Ham or game	Orange slices
Pork or veal roast	Stewed prunes stuffed with walnut
Roast	Broiled peach or pear halves filled with tart jelly
Meat loaf or jellied meats	Wedges or slices of hard-cooked eggs dusted with paprika
Creamed dishes	Fried tomato slices
Roasts, steaks and chops	Onions stuffed with bread dressing and baked
Pork, ham, lamb or game	Preserved kumdquats
Anything	Pork, ham, lamb or game

TIME AND TEMPERATURE CHART
FOR ROASTING

CUT	TEMP.	WEIGHT		APPROXIMATE TIME
BEEF				
Standing Rib Roast	250	3 1/2 lb.	rare	50 min
			medium	80 min
			well done	90 min
		5 1/2 lb.	rare	40 min
			medium	60 min
			well done	75 min
		7 1/2 lb.	rare	30 min
			medium	45 min
			well done	50 min
		10 lb.	rare	18 - 25 min
			medium	22 - 35 min
			well done	35 - 40 min
	300	3 1/2	rare	35 min
			medium	47 min
			well done	55 min
		5 1/2	rare	32 min
			medium	45 min
			well done	54 min
		7 1/2	rare	27 min
			medium	34 min
			well done	39 min
	350	3 1/2	rare	27 min
			medium	38 min
			well done	43 min
		5 1/2	rare	25 min
			medium	30 min
			well done	34 min
		7 1/2	rare	21 min
			medium	26 min
			well done	29 min
Chuck Rib	275 - 300			30 - 40 min
Rump	275 - 300			30 - 40 min
Boned Roast				add 10-15 min
Tongue	250 - 350			1 1/2 to 2 hrs.
Heart	250 - 300			2 1/2 to 3 hrs.
Meatloaf	300 - 350			1 1/2 to 2 hrs.

Time and Temperature Chart for Roasting Cont.

HAM, cured		
Whole	250 - 300	25 - 30 min
Half	250 - 300	35 - 40 min
Shank end	250 - 300	40 - 45 min
Butt end	300 - 350	40 - 45 min
Cured whole tender	300 - 325	20 -25 min
LAMB		
Leg	250 - 300	30 - 35 min
Shoulder	250 - 350	30 - 35 min
Shoulder, rolled	250 - 300	40 - 45 min
Breast	275 - 300	45 - 50 min
Loaf	300 - 325	30 min
VEAL		
Leg roast	250 - 300	25 - 35 min
Loin	250 - 300	30 - 45 min
Rack, 4-6 ribs	250 - 300	30 - 45 min
Shoulder	300	25 - 35 min
Shoulder, rolled	250 - 300	40 - 55 min
PORK, FRESH		
Ham	300 - 350	40 - 50 min
Loin	300 - 350	35 - 50 min
Butt	300 - 350	40 - 50 min
Spare rib	300	1 1/2 hrs.
FISH		
Whole	350	15 - 18 min
Steaks	350	45 - 60 min
CHICKEN	250 - 350	25 - 45 min
DUCK	250 - 350	25 - 30 min
TURKEY		
7 - 10 lbs. drawn	250 - 300	30 - 35 min
10 - 15 lbs. drawn	250 - 300	20 - 25 min
15 - 20 lbs. drawn	250 - 300	18 - 23 min
GOOSE		
10 lbs. young	250 - 300	25 - 28 min

* Roasting charts can only be approximate

TIME AND TEMPERATURE CHART
FOR BROILING

The following times can be used only as a guide due to variations in 1) quality of meat, 2) thickness, 3) temperature of meat, 4) desired degree of doneness, 5) position of pan, 6) length of flame.

Place food on cold pan. Place 1 to 4 inches from flame. Close door. Broil first half of time, turn. Broil for last half of time.

Cut	Thickness	Rare in minutes	Medium in minutes	Well done minutes
BEEF:				
Loin Steaks	1 inch	6 to 12	12 to 20	20 to 25
Rib Steaks	1 inch	6 to 12	12 to 20	20 to 25
Short Ribs				45 to 80
Liver	3/4 inch		10 to 15	
Sweet Breads				12 to 20
Ground Beef Patties	1 inch	6 to 12	12 to 20	20 to 25
Meat Loaf	2 inches			25 to 35
Frankfurters				12 to 20
LAMB:				
Chops, steaks, patties	1 inch		12 to 15	15 to 20
PORK:				
Fresh				
Sausage, links or patties				15 to 30
Spare Ribs				30 to 60
Cured Ham	1 inch			25 to 30
Ham-tender	1 inch			16 to 20
Bacon				2 to 5
FOWL:				
Chicken, halves-disjointed				
1 1/2 to 2 1/2 pounds				20 to 45
Turkey, disjointed				
3 to 5 pounds				20 to 45
Guinea, 2 to 3 pounds				20 to 45
FISH:				
Steaks				10 to 30
Whole Fish				20 to 40
Oysters				6 to 15

61

FISH HINTS

- **To make fish firm and white:** Add a little lemon juice to water while boiling.

- **To avoid unpleasant odors while cooking fish**: Cover with browned butter or lemon juice.

- **To remove fish odors from cooking utensils**: Add 2 tablespoons ammonia to the dish water.

- **To keep salmon and other fragile foods from breaking while being boiled**: Place food on a plate, tie in a square of cheese-cloth and lower all into water.

TEMPERATURES FOR BAKING FISH

Fish weighing from 3 to 5 pounds may be baked on heavy paper in a shallow pan or on a baking sheet, in a very hot oven for the first 10 to 15 minutes. Reduce temperature to 425 F. and bake 30 to 45 minutes longer. Allow 10 minutes for each of the first 4 pounds and 5 minutes for each dditional pound.

METHODS OF COOKING FRESHWATER FISH

Fresh Water Fish	Broil	Bake	Boil	Fry	Chowder
Blue Pike	yes	yes	no	yes	no
Buffalo Fish	yes	yes	no	yes	no
Carp	yes	yes	yes	yes	no
Catfish	no	no	yes	yes	yes
Crappy	yes	yes	no	yes	no
Lake Herring	yes	yes	no	yes	no
Lake Trout	yes	yes	yes	yes	no
Pickerel (Jacks)	yes	yes	no	yes	yes
Sauger	yes	yes	no	yes	no
Sheepshead	yes	yes	yes	yes	no
Smelt	yes	yes	no	yes	no
Suckers	yes	yes	no	yes	no
Whitefish	yes	yes	no	yes	no
Yellow Perch	yes	yes	no	yes	no
Yellow Pike	yes	yes	no	yes	no

Desserts

PIES, CAKES, ETC. HINTS

- **To prevent juices from cooking out of pies into oven**: Place a strip of dampened cloth or pastry tape around edge of pie; or place a tiny funnel or 4-inch stick of uncooked macaroni upright in center of the pie.

- **To avoid shrinkage of pie crust**: Roll pastry, place in pie-pan without stretching and set aside 5 minutes before fluting the edge. Or place another pie-pan on pastry before baking. Remove after 15 minutes of baking.

- **Line cake pans with plain or waxed paper**: Instead of greasing. Cut several pieces at one time to fit the bottom of pans and keep them on hand.

- **To grease pans easily**: Mix ½ cup shortening and ¼ cup flour to a smooth paste. Spread thinly on pans. Keep a supply of the mix in a covered dish to use when needed.

TEST FOR CAKES

Cakes are baked if:
- Cake tester or toothpick inserted in center of cake comes out clean.
- Cake shrinks from edges of pan.
- Cake springs back when touched lightly with finger.

Small cakes and cookies are baked if:
- They spring back from the finger touch and are brown.

63

When temperature is too high:
- Crust may be too dark.
- Pie may not be evenly baked.

When temperature is too low:
- Crust may be pale.
- Crust may be doughy.
- Filling may not be thoroughly cooked.

When pie is not baked long enough:
- Crust may be pale.
- Lower crust may be doiughy.

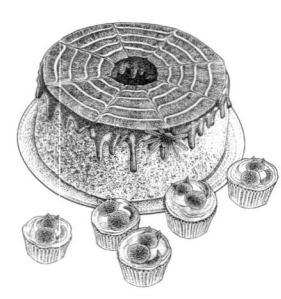

PASTRY AND CAKE BAKING ADVICE

PASTRY:

- **When pastry is rolled too thin**: It absorbs juices easily. It may not brown well. Top crust softens when pie cools. Crust breaks easily.
- **When pastry is rolled too thick:** It may not bake thoroughly.
- **When pastry is not properly fitted:** It may not brown evenly on bottom. Air under crust causes bubbles, making crust uneven. It may shrink during baking if stretched too much. Edge may become too brown if pastry is too far above pan.

FILLING:

- **When too much filling is used**: Juice may cook out into oven. Filling may not be thoroughly cooked.
- **When not enough filling is used:** Pie may be uneven in shape; lower in center than at sides.
- **When too much sugar is used**: It may be too sweet. It may be too syrupy, possibly cooking out into oven.
- **When not enough sugar is used**: Filling may be sour. May be too thin to serve nicely.

- **When too much thickening is used**: Filling may be pasty.
- **When not enough thickening is used**: Filling may be too juicy. Crust may soak. Pie is hard to serve.

CAKE BAKING:
- **If too much shortening is used**: Butter cakes may fall or fall apart.
- **If too little is used**: Butter cakes may have a tough crust, have too pale a crust, be tough or be dry.
- **If too soft**: Butter cakes may have soggy layers at bottom.
- **If liquid shortening is used**: Butter cakes may be coarse grained.
- **If too much sugar is used**: Butter cakes may fall, run over pan, have cracked crust, have moist crust, stick to pan have spongy layers at bottom fall apart. Sponge-cakes may fall, have a cracked crust, have a moist crust or stick to the pan.
- **If too little is used:** Butter cakes may have a tough crust, have too pale a crust or be tough or dry. Sponge-cakes have a tough crust, have too pale a crust, be tough or dry and or be too small.
- **If not creamed thoroughly with shortening**: Butter cakes may be course grained.

EGGS:
- **If beaten too much:** Sponge-cake will crack, hump or be tough.
- **If beaten too little:** Sponge-cake will be coarse grained.

EGG WHITES:
- **If beaten too much**: Butter cakes may be dry. Sponge cakes may be too small or be dry.
- **If beaten too little**: Sponge cakes may be too small.

EGG YOLKS:

- **If beaten too little:** Butter cakes may have soggy layers at bottom.   Sponge cakes may be too small or have soggy layers at bottom.

- **If too many are used in proportion to ingredients:** Sponge cakes may have soggy layers at bottom.

LEAVENING:

- **If too much is used**: Butter cakes may fall, run over pan, have too pale a crust, be coarse grained, be dry or fall apart.

- **If too little is used:** Butter cakes may be too small.

FLOUR:

- **If too much is used:** Butter cakes may crack or hump, have a tough crust or be dry. Sponge cakes may crack or hump, have a tough crust, have too pale a crust or be dry.

- **If it is damp:** Butter cakes may have a cracked crust, have moist crust or have soggy layers at bottom. Sponge cakes may have cracked crust or have moist crust.

- **If all-purpose flour is used:** Butter cakes may be coarse grained. Sponge cakes may be coarse grained.

LIQUID:

- **If too little is used:** Butter cakes may crack or hump or be dry.

- **If too much is used:** Butter cakes may have soggy layers at the bottom.

MIXING:

- **If over-mixed:** Butter cakes may be tough.Sponge cakes may be too small, fall, have tough crust or just be tough.

- **If not be mixed enough:** Butter cakes may have soggy layers at the bottom. Sponge cakes may have soggy layers at the bottom or be coarse grained.

CAKE PANS:
If too small: Butter cakes may run over pan. Sponge cakes may run over pan.

If too large: Butter cakes may be too flat.

TEMPERATURE:
If too high: Butter cakes may be too small, burn on sides, crack or hump, have a tough crust or just be tough. Sponge cakes may burn on sides, crack or hump, have a tough crust or be tough.

If too low: Butter cakes may run over pan, have too pale a crust, be coarse grained or be dry. Sponge cake may run over pan, have too pale a crust, be coarse grained or be dry.

BAKING TIME:
If too long: Butter cake may have a tough crust, have a hard crust or be dry. Sponge cake may have a hard crust or be dry.

If too short: Butter cake may fall or have a moist crust. Sponge cake may fall, fall apart or have a moist crust.

OVEN ARRANGEMENT:
If oven is too crowded: Butter cakes may rise unevenly or burn on sides. Sponge cakes may rise unevenly or burn on sides.

COOKIE BAKING TEMPERATURES

Slow: 300° F.: Cookies which bake without browning. Some macaroons, some rolled wafers. Cookies using egg for a large part of the liquid.

Moderately Slow: 325° F.: Most cookies containing fruit, molasses, oatmeal or chocolate.

Moderate: 350° F.: Some fruit, nut or molasses cookies.

Moderately Hot: 375° F.: Most rolled and molded cookies. Filled cookies. Most drop cookies unless rich in fruit or make with molasses.

Hot: 400° F.: Some refrigerator cookies.

TIME AND TEMPERATURES
FOR BAKED GOODS

Baking Times at Preheated Oven Temperatures

	Temperature setting (F.)	Time (minutes)
BREADS		
baking powder biscuits	450	12 to 15
breads	400	20
	then 350	40 to 50
coffee bread	375 - 400	20 to 25
coffee cake	400	30
corn bread	400	30
fruit or nut bread	350	60
muffins	425	20 to 30
popovers	450	20
	then 350	15 to 20
rolls	400 - 425	15 to 20
spoon	350	35 to 45
CAKES		
Angel food	325	1 1/4 hours
Chocolate		
layer	350	25
square	325	60
Cupcake	375	20 to 25
Fruitcake		
steamed 1 hr. then baked		
light	250	1 hour
rich	250	3 hour
entirely baked	275 - 300	1 1/2 to 4 hrs.
Gingerbread	350	45 - 50
Jelly roll	350	15 - 20
Layer	375	25 - 30
Loaf (deep)	325 - 350	1 to 1 1/4 hrs.
Poundcake	275 - 325	1 to 2 hrs.
Spongecake	325	60
Square (shallow loaf)	350	50
Tortes	350	20 - 40
Upside-down cake	350	50
COOKIES		
Fruit, molasses or chocolate	325 - 350	12 to 15
Other drop and rolled	375 - 400	8 to 12
Other refrigerator (sliced)	400	8
Ladyfingers	350	10 to 12
Macaroons	300	30

MERINGUES		
	275	45 to 60
PASTRY		
Pie shells	400	15
Puff pastry	450 - 500	5 to 8
Puff shells		
cream puffs and eclairs	450	15
	then 350	20 to 25
tarts	450	10 to 15
turnovers	450	15
PIES		
deep-dish pies	450	10
	then 350	30 - 35
meat pies		
biscuit top	450	15 - 20
pastry	450	15
	then 350	30
meringues on cooked fillings	350	15 - 20
one-crust (unbaked)	450	10
	then 350	25 - 30

TEMPERATURES AND TESTS FOR CANDY AND FROSTINGS

Syrup: Thread stage 228 to 234 degrees F. spins a 2-inch thread, when dropped from spoon.

Fudge: Penuche, Frosting, Fondant; Soft-ball stage, 234 to 240 degrees F. When a small amount is dropped into cold water it forms a soft ball which flattens when removed.

Caramels: Firm-ball stage, 244 to 248 degrees F. When a small amount is dropped into cold water it forms a firm ball which does not flatten when removed.

Divinity, Nougat, Popcorn balls, Salt-water taffy: Hard-ball stage, 250 to 265 degrees F. When a small amount is dropped into cold water it forms a ball which holds its shape.

Butterscotch taffy, Pulled candies; Crack stage, 270 to 290 degrees F. When a small amount is dropped into cold water it separates into threads but is not brittle.

Brittle, Glace: Hard-crack stage, 295 to 310 degrees F. When a small amount is dropped into cold water it separates into hard brittle threads.

Caramel Burnt sugar: Clear to brown liquid, 310 degrees F. Becomes hard when cool.

Miscellaneous

INGREDIENT DEFINITIONS

FATS AND OILS

Butter: Fat from sour or ripened cream gathered in a mass, some times salted and colored.

Compound: A mixture of animal fats, a mixture of vegetable fats or a mixture of both.

Corn Oil: Refined oil from the dried, crushed corn germ.

Cottonseed Oil: Refined oil from the crushed seed of the cotton plant.

Crackilins: The residue from rendered fat of meat or poultry.

Cream: The fat of milk that rises to the top when it stands.

Drippings: The fat obtained from cooking meats

Hydrogenated Fats: Oils or soft fats changed to solid fat by treat ment with hydrogen.

Lard: Fat rendered from the fatty tissues of the hog.

Nut Margerine: Made from nut oils: coconut, peanut or palm oil.

Oleomargerine: Made by churning a mixture of oils, milk and salt to a consistency similar to butter.

Olive Oil: Oil from flesh of ripe olives. Virgin olive oil is that which is first extracted and is better in flavor and appearance than the oil produced by the second or third pressing.

Peanut Oil: The oil extracted from peanuts. A by-product of peanut butter.

Suet: Clear, white fat of beef and mutton, usually from around the heart or kidney.

Sweet Butter: Made from sweet cream. Unsalted.

Vegetable Oil: Refers to oils extracted from several sources.
  a) Canola oil; the healthiest choice today. It is cholesterol free, only has 1 gram of fat and has 50% less saturated fat than olive or other oils. It ranks third in consumption.
  b) Soybean oil; accounts for about half of all edible oil produced.
  c) Corn oil is one of the most common and inexpensive cooking oils.
  d) Other vegetable cooking oils in order of consumption are; Palm oil, Sunflower oil, Cottonseed oil, Peanut oil and Olive oil.

Whipped Butter: Butter into which air has been whipped.

FLOUR

All Purpose Flour: A blend of hard or soft wheat flours. It can be used with good results for all types of baking.

Bran: A by-product of whole wheat flour. It contains some of the outer husk and some of the endosperm.

Bread Flour: Milled from inner part of hard or spring wheat.

Buckwheat Flour: Milled from the finely ground buckwheat kernel.

Cake Flour: Milled from soft wheat, the most highly refined flour milled; granulation uniform; protein content very low and also very delicate in quality.

Corn Meal: Milled from corn.

Graham or Whole-Wheat Flour: Milled from cleaned whole-wheat grain.

Pastry Flour: Usually made of soft wheat; low in protein and finely milled, though not as fine as cake flour.

Rice Flour: Milled from rice.

Rye Flour: Milled from rye grain. More like wheat flour in bread making qualities than any other grain.

Self-rising Flour: Milled from soft or winter wheat and has salt and leavening added.

Soybean Flour: Milled from the soybean.

MILK

Buttermilk: The product remaining after fat has been removed from sweet or sour milk or cream in the process of churning.

Certified Milk: Milk produced under carefully controlled hygienic conditions so it has a low bacteria count. Usually pasteurized.

Cultured buttermilk: Product made by souring pasteurized skimmed milk with a suitable culture of lactic acid bacteria.

Dry Milk: Milk from which all the water has been removed. Sold in powdered form.

Evaporated Milk: Milk from which more than half of the water has been removed by heating in a vacuum. It is homogenized, canned, then sealed in sterilized containers.

Homogenizing Process: Mechanical treatment of milk reducing the size and increasing the number of fat globules. Cream does not rise to the surface after this treatment but remains dispersed throughout the milk.

Irradiated Evaporated Milk: Milk which is treated after evaporation with ultraviolet rays to increase the Vitamin D content, then homogenized and sealed.

Malted Milk: Product made by drying a combination of whole milk and liquid separated from a mash of ground barley malt and wheat flour. It may contain sodium chloride, sodium bicarbonate or potassium bicarbonate.

Pasturized Milk: Milk that has been heated to a temperature not lower than 142 degrees F. for 30 minutes to destroy bacteria, then cooled at once to 50 degrees or lower.

Skimmed Milk: Portion of milk remaining after part or all of cream has been removed.

Sour Cream: Cream which is soured naturally by the action of lactic acid bacteria or by the addition of lemon juice or vinegar.

Sour Milk: Milk soured naturally by the action of lactic acid bacteria or by theaddition of lemon juice or vinegar

Sweetened Condensed Milk: Sweetened whole milk from which a large amount of water has been evaporated.

Vitamin D Milk: Milk with increased Vitamin D content.

CARE OF MILK IN THE HOME:

Take milk into the house and place it in the refrigerator as soon as possible. Place the milk in the coldest part of the refrigerator at once. Return milk to refrigerator as soon as the amount needed has been removed. Keep milk closely covered as it absorbs odors from other foods easily.

SPICES AND HERBS

All Spice: The dried berry of pimento trees, the flavor resembles a combination of cloves, cinnamon and nutmeg.

Anise: A licorice-like flavor. Lightly used in cookies, candies, cakes and breads.

Balm: A sharp lemon scent. Use fresh or dried in soups and salads.

Basil: With a gentle Mediterranean flavor similar to cloves it is often used in tomato recipes. Excellent to use with almost all vegetables except potatoes

Bay Leaves: A woodsy flavor. Excellent in soups, sauces, pot roast, sauerbraten and stews.

Capers: The pickled buds of a spiny shrub that bears rounded, fleshy leaves and big white to pinkish-white flowers. Used as a condiment.

Caraway: Taste like celery and is aromatic with a slight bitterness which enhances other flavors.

Cardamom: An aromatic fruit. The fruit is in the shape of a pod with seeds inside. Sold in the whole pod, as whole seeds or as ground seeds. Used as a condiment.

Cayenne Pepper: Powdered pod and seeds of various red peppers, it has a hot savory flavor. Used in meat dishes and gravies.

Celery Salt: A mixture of ground celery seed and fine white salt. Used in meats, salads and many other dishes.

Celery Seed: Taste like celery and is aromatic with a slight bitterness which enhances other flavors.

Chervil: An apiaceous plant with aromatic leaves used to flavor soups and salads.

Chili: A hot pepper. Used as a base for chili sauce and other spicy dishes.

Chili Powder: A mixture of ground red peppers, cumin seed and other spices. Used to flavor omelet's, sea food, cocktails, etc.

Chives: Similar to green onions though smaller and milder.

Chocolate: The plastic or solid product derived from grinding cacao nibs.

Chutney: A spicy pickle of compound fruit and seasonings.

Cilarntro: With a pungent flavor and aroma it is used as a seasoning in stews, soups, vegetables, salads, relishes and tomato based sauces.

Cinnamon: True cinnamon is the inner bark of Cinnamon zeylancium which grows only in Ceylon. It has a very mild flavor. Cassia cinnamon grown also in the Far East is most generally used and has a more full-bodied flavor. The dried bark is sold in sticks or ground.

Cloves: The flower buds of a tree which is grown in the East Indies, Zanzibar and Madagascar. Sold whole or ground.

Cocoa: Pulverized chocolate from which part of the cacao butter has been removed.

Coriander: An herb with aromatic seeds. Used for confections, cookies, pickles and meat products.

Cuminseed: Has a slightly bitter flavor. Used for flavoring meats, sausages, pickles and as an ingredient of curry powder.

Curry Powder: A yellow seasoning from India containing various spices.

Dill: An herb grown for its aromatic seed. Used in pickles and sauces.

Dutch Cocoa: Has a rich dark color due to the alkalis or carbonates used in processing.

Fennel: Resembling celery in appearance it has a fragrance and taste similar to anise. The young stalks are used as a salad green or served like celery.

Filé Powder: A spice made from dried and ground sassafras leaves with a distinctive flavor and texture. Often used when making several types of gumbo as a seasoning and thickening agent.

Garlic: A strong flavored plant, the cloves are used to flavor meats, salads, etc.

Garlic Salt: A mixture of garlic and fine white salt used in meats, salads, etc.

Ginger *(fresh)*:Taste different than powdered ginger. The root has a bite, a sweetness and a woodsy aroma. It should not be used at the same time as powdered ginger.

Horseradish: Is a long, rough, tapering root. Dried, flaked and powdered, it will retain its pungency more fully than the grated form which is stored in vinegar. Once scraped or broken, it exudes a penetrating smell irritating to the nose and eyes. It has a very strong, very hot and sharp flavor

Leeks: A strong flavored plant similar to onion.

Licorice: Is the rhizome of a bean plant. It is available as dried, woody pieces of root, as a powder and as solid sticks of concentrated essence. It has a medicinal and highly aromatic odor. It also has a sweet taste with a slightly bitter, slightly salty aftertaste.

Mace: The aroma is similar to nutmeg but it has a different flavor. It is sold whole as "blades" or ground and is used to flavor sauces, gravies, cakes and pies.

Marjoram: A fragrant annual the leaves are dried and used whole or powdered to flavor soups, salads, stuffing's, meats and sausages.

Mincemeat Spice: A mixture of spices such as cloves, allspice, cinnamon, etc. Used to flavor mincemeat, cakes, cookies and sauces.

Mint: A fragrant plant, the leaves are used (ether fresh or dried) to flavor soups, vegetables, fruits and beverages.

Mustard: A plant, the seeds are used either whole or ground. Combined with spices and vinegar it produces a product called prepared mustard. Used with meats, salads, etc.

Nutmeg: Sold whole or ground, it is the kernel of a fruit grown in the East and West Indies.

Onion: A strong flavored plant it is used to flavor meats, salads, etc.

Onion Salt: A dried mixture of onion and fine white salt used to flavor meats, soups and salads.

Oregano: Has a strong, spicy flavor and is used largely with Greek, Mexican and Italian cooking.

Panocha: Is brown Mexican sugar. It is sold in little pillars. Brown sugar may be substituted, but it's not as good.

Paprika: A bright red sweet pepper with a vibrant flavor; It is also known as pimient or tomato pepper and taste great with eggs, poultry, stew and vegetables.

Parsley: A herb used to flavor meats, vegetables and salads. Used also as a garnish.

Pectin Powder: Is a natural product found in the cell wall of all higher plants (citrus). It is a natural dietary source of fiber and is used for jellifying, thickening and stabilizing a variety of products in the food industry, such as jams and dairy products.

Pepper: Is the fruit, called peppercorns, from several species of plants. Black pepper, the most hot, is the dried, unripe berry. White pepper, less hot, starts out the same as the black, but is allowed to ripen on the vine. Green pepper, the least hot, is from the same fruit but is harvested before they mature. Pepper flavor and odor is very pungent and fiery.

Pimiento: The fleshy fruit of the Spanish paprika. Canned and used in meat and vegetable dishes and salads.

Poppy Seed: Used for breads, rolls, cakes and cookies. Oil may be extracted and used in a salad oil.

Poultry Seasoning: A mixture of spices such as sage, thyme, marjoram, etc.

Pumpkin Pie Spice: A mixture of spices such as cinnamon, cloves, ginger, etc.

Rose Hip: Are merely the seed pods formed after the rose blooms fade away. They have been used as a source of Vitamin C. They are commonly used as an herbal tea, used in jam, jelly and marmalade, to make soup (especially popular in Sweden) and as a type of mead. Particularly high in Vitamin C they also contain vitamins D and E, iron, essential fatty acids and antioxidants. The powder is a remedy for rheumatoid arthritis. They are attributed with the ability to prevent urinary bladder infections and assist in treating dizziness and headaches.

Rosemary: A evergreen plant, the leaves and flowers are used to flavor and garnish fish, stew and sauces.

Saffron: Is the world's most expensive spice. It has a pungent bitter-honey taste and is strongly perfumed. Its most common function is to color rice yellow. Very little is required for cooking purposes and the key is to distribute it evenly throughout the dish being prepared.

Sage: Has a fragrant aroma and a warm flavor. Crumble leaves to get the full fragrance. Use it sparingly, the flavor of crumbled leaves are absorbed into foods more quickly than leaf Sage. Enhances the flavor of seafood, vegetables and breads.

Sausage Seasoning: A mixture of spices such as white pepper, coriander and nutmeg.

Savory: Has a clean, piney fragrance and peppery flavor. Enhancing almost any dish, it goes well with soups, stews, bean dishes and cabbage.

Scallions: Small onions.

Sesame Seed: Has a nut-like, mild flavor. It is used in breads, candies, main dishes, as a garnish on pasta and vegetables and for its oil content.

Soy Sauce: A highly flavored sauce made from fermented soybeans. It is used largely in oriental dishes.

Tabasco Sauce: A highly seasoned sauce made with cayenne peppers and other ingredients.

Tarragon: Has a slightly bittersweet flavor and an aroma similar to anise. Commonly known as a flavoring for vinegar, it also goes well with relishes, fish, meat, soups and stews. It also adds a distinctive flavor to sauces.

Thyme: Has a subtle, dry aroma and a slightly minty flavor. It goes well with a variety of foods including poultry, seafood, soups, lamb and veal. It is often used with tomatoes.

Turmeric: Is mildly aromatic and has scents of orange or ginger. It has a pungent, bitter flavor. It is a necessary ingredient of curry powder. Used largely in Indian dishes, it is used in mustard blends and relishes. It is also used to provide color and flavor in place of saffron.

Vanilla: The beans have a sweet, perfumed aroma with a woody or smoky flavor. The extract has a similar aroma. Being one of the most popular flavorings in the world, it is used in desserts such as ice cream, cake, candy and pudding. It is also used to enhance the flavor of beverages and sauces.

Yerba Buena: Wild mint is strung, dried in the air and stored. The leaves are used for garnishing as well as flavoring.

SUGAR

Brown Sugar: Comes from the late stages of sugar refining, when sugar forms fine crystals with significant molasses-content, or from coating white refined sugar with a cane molasses syrup.

Confectioners' Sugar: Powdered sugar which has been sifted and made into a very fine powder.

Corn Sugar: Sugar manufactured from corn.

Cube Sugar: Crystals of granulated sugar pressed together into molds and cut into cubes.

Granulated Sugar: Refined into crystals or granulated form from either sugar cane or beets.

Maple Sugar: Crystallized maple syrup.

Powdered Sugar: Granulated sugar powdered by pressure.

SYRUPS

Cane Syrup: The concentrated sap of sugar cane.

Corn Syrup: Made from corn.

Crystal White Syrup: Corn syrup, granulated sugar and vanilla.

Golden Syrup: Corn syrup and refiner's syrup.

Flavored Syrup: Corn syrup with one or more of the following flavorings: maple, honey, sorghum and butterscotch.

Honey: A syrupy sweet material out of nectar of flowers, elaborated in honey sac of the honey bee and stored in their nests.

Maple Syrup: The concentrated sap of the maple tree.

Molasses: Is a thick syrup by-product from the processing of the sugarcane into sugar. The quality depends on the maturity of the sugar cane, the amount of sugar extracted and the method of ex traction. Used to make industrial alcohol and rum products it can also be used to make yeast, cure tobacco and in cattle feed.

Refiners' Syrup: The liquor obtained in the process of refining sugar.

Sorghum Syrup: Sorghum and molasses are not the same. Molasses is a by- product of the sugar industry. Sorghum is the juice from the sorghum cane that is boiled to produce the syrup. It is very healthy containing iron, calcium and potassium. It does not need to be refrigerated but it could sugar. If this happens, just reheat it back to liquid form.

COOKING TERMS AND DEFINITIONS

Al Dente: To cook until tender but still slightly firm.

Appetizer: A small serving of food or beverage served before or as the first course of a meal.

Aspic: A transparent jelly made of stock, which has been boiled down sufficiently to become firm when cold. Also applies to meat, fish or vegetable stock which has been thickened with gelatin.

Au Jus: With natural juice.

Au Gratin: Covered with cheese or crumbs or both and baked.

Baste: To moisten food while baking with juices from pan or other liquid or fat.

Bake: To cook by dry heat in an oven. When meat is cooked uncovered it is referred to a roasting.

Bake Until Tender: Until a fork or skewer can easily be inserted.

Barbecue: To roast or broil, usually revolving over hot coals, while basting with a highly seasoned vinegar sauce. Other methods exist depending on what part of the country you're in.

Batter: A thin mixture of flour and liquid, usually combined with other ingredients.

Beat: To mix ingredient with a spoon wire whip or rotary beater.

Bisque: A rich thick cream soup usually made from fish. Also a rich frozen dessert, usually containing powdered nuts or macaroons.

Blanch: To quickly immerse vegetables or fruit into boiling water for 1 to 2 minutes then into cold water to stop the cooking process. It is also helpful in removing skins from tomatoes or peaches.

Blend: To thoroughly mix two or more ingredients.

Boil: To cook in a liquid hot enough for bubbles to break the surface and steam to be given off.

Bonbon: A sweet made of or dipped into fondant.

Bouillabaise: A chowder made of several varieties of fish and white wine.

Bouillon: A clear soup stronger than broth, yet not so strong as consommé.

Broil: To cook directly under a red hot heating unit, or over an open fire or grill.

Braise: Browning meat or poultry in a small amount of liquid or grease, then cooking, covered, over low heat for a long time. Good for cooking less tender cuts of meat.

Bread: To cover meat, poultry or fish with a dry covering. Usually seasoned flour, cracker or bread crumbs.

Brown: To cook in a small amount of grease over medium heat until the surface is browned. (Food may not be thoroughly cooked.)

Brush: To spread thinly with a brush or finger.

Café Au Lait: Equal parts of coffee and milk.

Caffeine: An alkaloidal substance found in the coffee bean, coffee leaf, tea leaf, cacao-bean, etc.

Canape: An appetizer made of a small piece of bread spread with a highly seasoned food.

Capon: A castrated male chicken. Grows large and has tender meat.

Caramel: Burnt sugar syrup used for coloring and flavoring. Also a chewy candy.

Caramelize: Sugar melted to a golden brown.

Caviar: Salted roe (fish eggs). Originally from sturgeon.

Charlotte: Usually a gelatin dessert with flavored whipped cream molded in a form lined with cake or ladyfingers.

Chicory: The root of a plant that is cut into slices, dried and roasted as coffee. Leaves of the plant are used for salads and sometimes called curly endive.

Chill: To become completely cold but not frozen.

Chop: Cutting into coarse or fine pieces.

Cider: The juice pressed from apples used as a beverage or to make vinegar.

Coat: Covering a food with an ingredient such as flour or sauce.

Coats A Spoon: Refers to the stage of cooking a sauce or custard where a film forms on a metal spoon.

Cobbler: A deep-dish fruit pie with a rich biscuit dough used instead of pastry dough.

Cocktail: (a) An appetizer served before or as the first course of a meal. (b) An alcoholic beverage usually served before dinner. (c) Fruit or vegetable juice. (d) Cut fruit or shellfish with tart sauce served as first course.

Combine: The mixing of ingredients.

Compote: Sweetened stewed fruit, cooked to keep the fruit as whole as possible.

Condiments: Food seasonings such as salt, vinegar, herbs and spices.

Consomme: A highly seasoned clear soup made from one or a combination of meats.

Cracklings: Crisp particles left after fat has been fried out.

Cream: To soften butter, shortening or lard by rubbing it against the bowl with a spoon or beating with an electric mixer until it is light and creamy.

Cream Sauce: A white sauce made with cream.

Cream Together: To blend two or more ingredients together until they are light and fluffy

Crisp-tender: Cooking until tender but not soft or limp. (Such as vegetables)

Croquettes: A mixture of chopped or ground cooked food held together by eggs or a thick sauce, shaped, dipped into egg and crumbs and fried.

Croustade: A French term meaning a crust or pie-crust of any type. Usually made of flaky pastry or puff pastry. There are also bread, potato and other croustades.

Croutons: Cubes of toasted or fried bread served with soup.

Cube: To cut into solids of 6 equal square sides.

Custard: A cooked or baked mixture mainly of eggs and milk. It may be sweetened to use as a dessert or flavored with cheese, fish, etc., as an entrée.

Cut In: To combine shortening, butter or lard with dry ingredients using two knives, a fork or pastry blender.

Cutlet: A small piece of meat cut from the leg or rib of veal or pork.

Dash: About half of 1/8 teaspoon of a spice or seasoning.

Dice: To cut into small cubes.

Deep-dish Pie: A fruit pie with top crust only, baked in a deep dish.

Deep-fry: Cooking food in enough hot grease to cover the food.

Deglaze: Adding (usually wine, brandy, juice or broth) to a hot pan after sautéing or roasting to release the meat's essence left in the pan.

Dilute: Thinning a liquid or reducing flavor by adding a liquid

Dissolve: To make a product melt or liquefy.

Dough: A mixture of liquid, flour, etc, that is stiff enough to be handled or kneaded.

Dredge: To lightly cover a food with flour or other ingredient.

Drippings: Fat and liquid resulting from cooking meat.

Drizzle: To pour a liquid over food in a fine stream.

Dust: To sprinkle or coat lightly with flour or sugar.

Entrée: The main dish of an informal meal or a subordinate dish served between main courses.

Flake: To break into small pieces with a fork.

Flute/fluting: To press or crimp an edge into a piecrust before baking, using a fork, finger or fluting tool.

Fold: Combining a light ingredient with another heavier ingredient by gently turning the mixture with a spoon or spatula. Such as to mix fruit into muffin or pancake batter.

Fold In: To mix by gently cutting down through and bringing up close to the bowl, then folding over before cutting down through again. Proper folding prevents loss of air.

Fondant: A sugar and water mixture cooked to the soft-ball stage (234 degrees F.), cooled and kneaded.

Fondue: A light preparation of cheese and eggs.

Frappe: Partly frozen

Fricassee: A dish of any boiled meat served in a rich milk sauce.

Fritters: Fruit, meat, vegetables or fish covered with batter or chopped and mixed with batter. Usually deep-fried

Frosting:A cooked or uncooked sugar mixture used to cover cakes, cookies and other foods.

Fry:To cook in hot grease: Deep Fry…to cook in hot grease deep enough to float the food. Pan Fry…to cook in a small amount of grease. Often called sauté.

Garnish: An edible decoration added to a finished dish or dessert.

Gelatin: A purified protein found in connective tissues and bones of animals

Giblets:The heart, liver and gizzard of poultry.

Glaze Or Glace: Iced or glossed over. Meats are glazed by covering with concentrated stocks or jellies. Fruits may be frozen or covered with a shiny film of hardened sugar syrup

Goulash: A thick meat stew originating in Hungary.

Grate: To rub against a grater to tear food into bits or shreds of various sizes.

Grease:To rub the surface of a pan or dish with grease to prevent food from sticking.

Grease And Flour:To grease a pan and then lightly dust with flour, corn meal or other fine ingredient, to keep food from sticking.

Grill: To cook food on a rack over hot charcoal, a gas grill or other similar heat source.

Grind: To change a food into tiny particles by cutting and crushing in a food grinder.

Hollandaise: A rich sauce made of eggs and butter, served hot with vegetables and fish.

Hors D'oeuvres: Appetizing side dishes such as olives, radishes, celery and pickles.

Ice: A frozen mixture of fruit juice, sugar and water.

Infusion: Liquid extracted from coffee, tea or herbs.

Julienne: Food cut into fine strips or strings.

Knead: To place dough on a flat surface and work it, pressing down with knuckles, then fold over, repeating several times.

Leaven (Or Leavening): An ingredient that is used in dough and batters that causes a foaming action, such as baking powder, baking soda, buttermilk, sourdough starter or yeast,. When a dough or batter is baked, it "sets" and holes, left by the gas bubbles, remain giving baked goods their texture.

Lukewarm: Liquids and food that feel neither hot nor cold.

Macedoine: A mixture of vegetables or fruits.

Marinade: A seasoned liquid in which foods are soaked.

Marinate: To allow food to stand in a dry or liquid dressing or syrup to improve flavor.

Marzipan: A paste of sweet almonds and sugar.

Meringue: A mixture of stiffly beaten egg whites, flavoring and sugar.

Microwave: An oven that uses high-frequency radio waves to cook food quickly.

Mince: To cut with a knife or scissors into very tiny pieces.

Minestrone: A thick Italian vegetable soup.

Mix: To combine two or more ingredients.

Mocha: A flavoring made with coffee infusion or with an infusion of coffee and chocolate.

Mousse: A mixture of whipped cream, sugar and flavoring, frozen without stirring. Or flavored thin cream and gelatin combined with meat, fruits or vegetables.

Muffin: A drop batter baked in individual pans and served as a quick bread.

Panbroil: Cooking food, uncovered, over high heat on a hot surface, pouring off grease as it forms.

Panfry: Cooking food, uncovered, over high heat in a small amount of grease.

Parfait: A frozen dessert usually made with ice cream and syrup served in a parfait glass.

Parboil: To boil food in water until partially cooked.

Pare: To cut off the outside covering with a knife, as from a potato or apple.

Paring: To remove the outer covering or skin on a fruit or vegetable. Usually done with any small knife or potato peeler.

Peel: To remove outside covering by stripping off, as from a tomato, peach or banana.

Poach: To cook by surrounding with simmering (not boiling) water or other liquid.

Preheat: To turn on the heat in an oven and heat to the desired temperature before putting in the food.

Punch Down: Pushing down risen yeast dough to allow smaller, more uniform air pockets to form.

Puree: Food boiled to a pulp and put through a sieve.

Ragout: A thick highly seasoned stew.

Reconstitute: Adding water to dried or concentrated foods to restore them to their original consistency.

Reduce: Boiling a liquid to reduce the volume.

Rehydrate: Restoring water lost during drying by soaking or by cooking the food in liquid.

Relish: A highly seasoned food used as an accompaniment.

Roast: Cooking foods in an uncovered pan in the oven at moderate heat.

Roe: Fish eggs.

Roux: A cooked mixture of flour and butter: used as a base for gravy, sauces, soufflés, soups and stews.

Rub: A combination of different dry seasonings rubbed into meat and allowed to stand to improve flavor.

Saute: To cook gently in a small amount of fat or shortening.

Scald: To heat to just below boiling point.

Scallop: Layering sliced food with a sauce or other liquid and baking in a casserole. (Usually potatoes)

Score: To cut narrow grooves or gashes.

Sear: To brown the surface quickly with intense heat.

Shred: To tear or cut into small, long, narrow pieces.

Sift: To pass through a sieve.

Simmer: To cook in liquid just below the boiling point.

Skewer: A long strong pin of wood or metal used to hold food together while cooking.

Slice: To cut into slices

Sliver: To cut or shred into long pieces.

Steam: To cook in the steam which arises from a pan of boiling water or other liquid.

Steep: To extract flavor or color from a food by placing the food in a heated liquid that is below the boiling point.

Stew: To cook slowly in a small amount of liquid for a long time.

Stir: To mix by rotary motion

Stir-Fry: Frying thinly and uniformly sliced food quickly in a small amount of hot liquid stirring constantly.

Stock: The juice left after roasting (meat or poultry), usually with water.

Strain/Drain: Removing liquid from food by allowing the excess liquid to drain out.

Thicken: To thicken a hot liquid or broth by adding a thin mixture of cornstarch and water, flour or arrowroot and stirring constantly.

Toasting: A technique where low to medium heat is applied in a dry skillet or baking pan to seeds, such as sesame, cumin and fennel, to release their aroma and flavor.

Toss: Gently mixing ingredients together by turning them over using two forks or a fork and a spoon.

Whip: Rapidly beating ingredients with a whisk, fork, or mixer in order to incorporate air into them until they are light and fluffy.

CARE OF KITCHEN UTENSILS

Aluminum: Wash with soap and water and scour to remove spots. Dry thoroughly after washing.

Chrome: Wash with soap and water and polish with a dry soft cloth.

Copper: Wash lacquered copper with soap and water and dry thoroughly. Polish unlacquered copper with a copper polish, wash with soap and water and dry thoroughly.

Enamel: Treat as glassware.

Glass Glass made especially for cooking and baking needs little care except washing with soap and water. When spots are hard to remove rub with scouring pads or a fine cleansing powder.

Iron: Wash with soap and water. Avoid scouring. Dry thoroughly after washing.

Nickel: Wash with soap and water. Polish with dry cloth.

Plastic: Wash with soap and water and scour to remove spots. Dry thoroughly after washing.

Steel: Wash with soap and water and scour to remove spots. Dry thoroughly after washing.

Tin: Wash with soap and water and scour with mild cleansing powders. Tin rusts easily so dry thoroughly after washing.

Wood: Scrape with dull blade and wash with lukewarm water. After removing cooked foods from utensils pour hot water into them, cover and set aside. This will loosen any food that has stuck to them. Do not soak wooden utensils.